A Peace Corps Profile

By Kirk A. Hackenberg

National Library of Canada Cataloguing in Publication

Hackenberg, Kirk A., 1952-
 A Peace Corps profile / Kirk A. Hackenberg.
ISBN 1-55369-676-X
 1. Hackenberg, Kirk A., 1952-. 2. Peace Corps
(U.S.)--Biography. I. Title.
HC60.5.H32 2002   361.6   C2002-902893-0

Printed in Victoria, Canada

TRAFFORD

This book was published *on-demand* in cooperation with Trafford Publishing.
On-demand publishing is a unique process and service of making a book available for retail sale to the public taking advantage of on-demand manufacturing and Internet marketing.
On-demand publishing includes promotions, retail sales, manufacturing, order fulfilment, accounting and collecting royalties on behalf of the author.

Suite 6E, 2333 Government St., Victoria, B.C. V8T 4P4, CANADA
Phone   250-383-6864   Toll-free   1-888-232-4444 (Canada & US)
Fax   250-383-6804   E-mail   sales@trafford.com
Web site   www.trafford.com   TRAFFORD PUBLISHING IS A DIVISION OF TRAFFORD HOLDINGS LTD.
Trafford Catalogue #02-089   www.trafford.com/robots/02-0489.html

10   9   8   7   6   5   4

*To my wife Gloria who sacrificed
so much to go through life by my side.*

*To my sons Kirk and Leo, who
mean the world to me.*

.

Acknowledgments

First and foremost I have to thank Linda Adams who was patient and persistent in getting me to write this account. I also have to thank her for all her time listening and encouraging me to continue even when I felt no one would want to read it. I have to thank both Linda and her son Casey Adams whom gave of their talents for grammatical structure and opinions on what could or shouldn't be included.

I would like to thank the Peace Corps for giving me the opportunity to serve.
(www.peacecorps.gov)

I would like to thank the Peace Corps Partnership Program for helping to fund my overseas projects.

I would like to thank the Foster Parents Plan for allowing me to contribute to children overseas.

Foreword

I have heard, over the years, many people say it is unfortunate that there are less fortunate people in the world. I have further heard that what is the use, because there are so many, that surely nothing a single individual could do would make a difference. I have even heard in-country and returned Peace Corps volunteers say they didn't make a difference. I contend that if you affect even one individual's life, for one moment in time, you have made a difference.

The folk singer, John Denver, tried to develop a program to feed the hungry and felt it was possible. Michael Jackson created the song "Man in the mirror" about making a change by starting with your self. However, I think Phil Collins sums it up best in his song "Another day in paradise". You can make a difference if you only give it a try. One smile on one face, for one moment in time, will change that person's life then and there.

A Brief Moment In A Life Time

I cannot tell you what it takes to become a Peace Corps volunteer, what traits or ambitions you need to have, and I don't profess to understand why I joined or why others do.

I can only give you a glimpse of my life, my reasons and what moved me to join. I would not say that I am an exceptional person or different from most others but maybe my reasons are best explained by a synopsis of my life up to the point of volunteering.

* * * *

In grade school, I always made friends with the children that stood apart from the group. Not the popular kids, but the ones that were made fun of because they were over weight, wore glasses, or the ones that were too weak to defend themselves. An example of one close friend was a boy in grade school that had polio and wore braces on both legs.

To me he was special, not because no one wanted to play with him, but because making him feel good about himself and seeing him laugh was more rewarding to me than enjoying the playground with the other children.

Even back then, at that young age, I would wonder if he would ever live a full life and how difficult would it be for him.

* * * *

I am not sure what part of my desire to help people might have stemmed from the influence of both a grandmother who was a non-denominational minister who lived with us in her final years and my cousin Judy, the daughter of my aunt and uncle who were missionaries in the Southwest working with the Navaho Indians on a reservation.

Judy was roughly six years older than me and was my favorite cousin, although they did not visit us very often. She was always so kind and attentive toward me. I was always captivated by her stories of the poor Indian people and what it was like living on the reservation.

Judy seemed to be one of the most concerned and caring people I knew in those early years. I admired what she and her brothers were going through living with and helping the Indian people. It appeared to me that her family was doing what it took to live with and help poor people. I am not saying that, at the time, I would have desired to do that but just the same, I believe it had an influence on what I would do and think in later years.

* * * *

During my junior year in high school I became a janitor at one of the local middle schools and, in addition, parked cars for a country club at night. I saved my money for college but kept a little aside and adopted a child through the foster parents plan supporting a child in Ecuador.

This was something I would keep secret from everyone because I didn't think anyone would understand; yet I felt so good about doing it. It was something I had seen in a magazine where for a few pennies a day or the cost of a cup of coffee you could help feed, clothe and educate a child overseas. The idea and the concept seemed so simple that I could not fathom why any one wouldn't do this. After all, I knew people that spent more on dog food weekly than this would cost. It was so rewarding and fulfilling that I would repeat doing it again during my college years by supporting a little girl in Bolivia.

To this day, I still have their photos, which can be seen on the back cover of this account with Benito of Ecuador to my left and Ruth of Bolivia to my right. Often times, during the Peace Corps years I thought how wonderful it would have been to visit them. They were young adults by then and I figured I now knew enough Spanish to have been able to speak with them.

It was very rewarding getting the photos and letters that were sent on behalf of the children and hearing about what clothing I helped buy or what went on in their school and family life.

* * * *

College was about learning how to deal with living on my own, what to make of my self and personal relationships. I entered not knowing what to major in, as was the case for most beginning students.

During my second year, I took a child psychology course. My professor suggested that I volunteer at the local elementary school to be of service and enhance my studies. Because the school was nearby and I could walk to it, I would assist in between my classes.

At first I would work with the slow learners in a tutoring role. I seemed to have a knack, or gift, for explaining things in ways children could understand. However, there were always children who seemed to be on the "outside looking in". I would sit with them, talk to them, and listen to what they had to say. My experience and research into the minds of those children became a mission to try to understand the loneliness and pain they must have felt, and to help them understand it as well.

I remember utilizing ideas from the program that Art Linkletter used to have, which I watched every chance I got, called "Children Say the Darndest Things". From that, I would do word association with the children to explore what their feelings were.

Consequently, I decided to become a child psychologist to help children.

* * * *

After the spring semester of my second year in college, I volunteered to work at a summer camp with mentally handicapped children.

Dale, another volunteer, and I got the idea to make a film about the center that could be shown to parents and teachers to help promote the activities there.

The art teacher brought in her camera and financed the film for Dale and me to proceed. We filmed, cut, and spliced. I took Cat Stevens music and dubbed the sound for "Where do the Children Play" along with some other tunes.

We completed the film in and around our other activities and showed it the final night of the program. The film, the music, and content, ended up getting Dale and me a standing ovation.

I learned then that if your creativity is tried to its limits something good can come from any situation no matter how difficult you might think it is. This idea would become the inspiration behind many of the activities I would one day do in the Peace Corps. While I found the experience rewarding, I knew immediately that I could not work with these special children on a long-term basis.

I just did not have what it took. It was a significant blow to my hopes and aspirations of maybe having found what it was that I would do with my life.

For the first time, I felt maybe I could not make a difference in a child's life.

* * * *

By the third year of college I was living and working in a center for emotionally disturbed children. I loved that work so much that I was only able to carry twelve semester hours to stay as active as I could at the center and still be a full time student.

I was also in love with a girl I met when she came to play guitar for the Sunday church sessions held at the center. The children at the center became my life and I devoted every bit of energy into helping them.

While all the children were important to me, two in particular, won my affection for different reasons. One boy at the center had a phobic neurosis and was afraid of every thing from closed doors to rain.

I remember one night hearing him crying because a thunderstorm had him nearly paralyzed with fear. I spent the night talking him through it and telling him of the little animals and insects that were having a party because they so badly needed the rain. We could hear the chirping of the crickets as the rain subsided. His eyes lit up and he became excited to think that the thing he feared really was a good thing.

We spent each subsequent day talking about each of his fears and addressed the positive things that would make the fears seem unimportant or at least not so frightening for him.

The boy's psychiatrist, who visited the center and only saw him once a month, and with whom I lived at the time, announced his successful work with that child the following month and attributed it to his psychotherapy. I knew better and felt a great deal of reward in what I was doing.

* * * *

Another child at the center who tore at my heart was a little girl that had been sexually molested, orphaned, and terrified of males. I was the only male at the center that she would come near, so the center personnel encouraged the contact between us.

After three months, I was allowed to take her out horseback riding with one of the female counselors. We progressed slowly with more and more outings to different places with the intent to get to the point of a weekend off campus, which she had never experienced since the time of her arrival some years earlier. As the weekends came and went, someone came to pick up most every other child for outings yet no one ever came for her. The look in her eyes, watching the other children leave, was truly heart breaking. You have seen this happen in many movies but in real life it is sadder than what any movie can portray.

When the big day came for me to take her alone all night off center, she was terrified. I had an apartment by this time and she was given my spare room to sleep in. She spent most of the night awake, crying and wetting the bed. After a number of subsequent visits her trust in me was established. She slept, and seemed to be doing well. I worked so hard with her, and we became such close friends, that I considered adopting her as a single parent.

My friends warned me against this. They said it would ruin my life having a child at my young age, and how was I ever to get a potential mate to accept me with a child.   These same friends thought I was becoming "weird" and told me they thought I needed a rest from working with children.

* * * *

I graduated as a child psychologist in 1975 from the University of Texas and applied for jobs all over the area.   As fate would have it the first thing I found was an offer of working with mentally handicapped adults as a cottage supervisor. This was something I knew I could not do. It would have required living in the complex and assisting them through their daily routines.

Instead, I took a job working in the laboratory of a meat packing plant. This was not because I was the best qualified for the job, but because I made it through the plant tour without throwing up. The guy that was better qualified could not accomplish this feat.

Those first weeks on the job without the companionship of fellow students in the college setting, and a crack forming in my love relationship, sent me into depression.

My reason for staying in the meat packing plant, and not pursuing my desires, was my love of Ruth. Deep down, maybe she realized that, or maybe because she needed time away from me, she decided to end our relationship.   One thing I knew for sure was that I could not bear to be in that city with the prospect of doing what did not matter to me, and not even with the comfort of the one I loved.

* * * *

I had always been curious about the Peace Corps. It sounded like it was sincere in trying to help people, so I got an application. I cannot say that my motivation was one concerned with helping people at the time. I was more motivated by wanting to escape my life.

I applied to the Peace Corps as a way out of a crippling hurt, and to get away from a town where her family had been mine. I applied to get away from a job I hated, and for what seems now, all the wrong reasons.

My Destiny

Getting the application for the Peace Corps was easy. All I had to do was go to the university where they were available, all eight or so pages.

I figured it was just a matter of telling them you wanted to join and off you went. Contrary to what I thought, Peace Corps, at the time of my interest, had targeted university graduates and was seeking people in health, education and agriculture, not just any one off the street. It wasn't as if people I knew were knocking down the doors to volunteer. After all, who would give up two years of their lives earning nothing while living in poverty?

Most of my peers were either getting married, or had started working and saving for a new car or a down payment on their house. I, however, in January of 1977 and just days after my 25th birthday was ready to do what others, including my parents, thought was nuts.

My friends and family thought I would be missing out on earning potential, losing another two years of possible spouse search, and all for what they believed was a hopeless cause anyway.

I even got into a heated argument with my closest friend while living in El Paso, Texas on the border of Mexico over the poor Mexican families living on the other side of the Rio Grande. We could see the mud and stick houses from where we went to swim.

My friend felt that there was no need to help them because according to him "they didn't know any better and therefore didn't know what they were missing and were content with their lives".

I, on the other hand, could not comprehend this type of mentality when certainly they could also look across the river at our houses and belongings. I believed we had a God given requirement to do our part to help others less fortunate. The irony of this was that his mother agreed with me and became the biggest supporter of my joining the Peace Corps and encouraged me to do so.

I would soon find out that the application process was very detailed with lots of essay questions, requests for references and, to some degree, a psychological profile of one's past. Indeed, the application process was designed such that anyone less than intent on going would not want to go to the level of effort and detail necessary to fill it out. I would venture to guess that by omitting items on the application gave the Peace Corps a step in screening the applicants. At the time I had no knowledge that for every vacancy available, there would be over a thousand applicants and I approached the process not the least bit worried. In fact, I quit my job at the meat packing plant prior to even hearing back from them. I had even arrogantly put on my application a preference of serving in Chile, South America. Was this over confidence of being accepted or a vision of my destiny?

The second stage of the process called for either a telephone interview for additional screening or one would be flown to Washington D.C. for a personal interview. I got neither.

What was more surprising was that within two weeks of quitting my job, I head from the Peace Corps. They wanted to send me to Swaziland, Africa. Even though I had traveled around Europe and studied geography in college, I had no idea where in Africa Swaziland was. In looking up information about the country at the library, and researching a little into the surrounding areas of that country, I found that the two countries bordering Swaziland were at war. Something inside of me said, "no, not yet".

I proceeded to let the Peace Corps know that while I did not want to go to Swaziland, I was still interested in an assignment.

What should have happened, and probably would have to any other individual, was to have been perceived as unwilling, uninterested, or not having serious intent, therefore, not being offered an assignment at all. The big shock came only one week later with offer of an assignment to Nicaragua, Central America. I said yes!

I accepted this offer for two basic reasons; first I figured if I turned this one down there would not be a third offer and second it was a Latin country. The love, the desire, and the draw that I had to getting to a Spanish speaking country was tied to the children I had fostered in the foster parents plan and Ruth, my now lost love, who had been born of full Hispanic heritage. I wanted to learn about their culture and language.

Peace Corps then sent the necessary documents to start the physical, dental and passport process prior to staging. While the passport and dental portion went without a hitch, the medical almost stopped the process.

It seems that I was born with a common condition that results in an opening in the spine. While not life threatening in any way, this could pose a medical problem if there was ever any continuous exposure to infectious conditions or if I was not careful in maintaining good physical hygiene.

Being able to maintain proper hygiene and/or get good medical attention could in some places be problematic. While the Peace Corps is willing to wave certain medical conditions, they will not accept volunteers who could potentially result in health risks overseas.

Again destiny would direct me and I was able to persuade the doctor to write into my file that the condition did not, in his opinion, need correction or feel it should warrant non-assignment. Anyway, the airline tickets arrived with my assignment to be in Miami, Florida for staging prior to being sent to Nicaragua. Imagine, never having direct contact with anyone from the Peace Corps and the next thing you know you are in a city you have never been to, preparing to go to a country you have never even visited, to work with people you have never met and to top it all off in a language you don't even speak.

* * * *

Peace Corps gave me a copy of recommended items to take and how many pounds of baggage I would be allowed. I went out and bought a zip-up sleeping jungle hammock, plenty of blue jeans and lots of deodorant.

Together with my cowboy boots from Texas, I could have passed for Indiana Jones at the time but the movie had not yet been made. I was significantly under the eighty-pound weight limit!

I boarded the plane without a second thought of what I was leaving, where I was going or what I was doing. I arrived in the Miami airport, took a taxi to the hotel the Peace Corps had arranged for us and found myself with a roommate.

My roommate was a minor league catcher for a baseball club and told me he was going to go down to Nicaragua and start a little league team. I looked at him in amazement, partly because I had no clue what I was going to do, and partly because I couldn't for the life of me figure out how his idea fit with what my vision of the Peace Corps was about.

I think he was just as puzzled about me not knowing what city I would be in, or what my job assignment was. Not trying to seem rude but more out of my logical curiosity, I asked him if he was going to introduce little league baseball to a small pueblo in the country where it did not exist, then, who were they going to play against? I could tell by the bewilderment on his face that he had not quite gotten into the reality of where he was going.

The entire staging group would meet the next day. There were roughly seventeen of us: old, young, men and women. We would go through the getting to know each other, what to expect when we arrived in the country, the language training, and which agency we would be working for; hence the word "staging".

The one part they didn't mention until the next day, and was painfully evident, was when the nurse showed up with the gamma globulin shots. This shot is in the butt cheek and feels like someone just inserted a balloon. We would have to go through a series of these and the first was prior to departure. Everyone was sitting funny by the afternoon session as though it was a hemorrhoid convention.

The most shocking thing about those three days in Miami was finding out that the first three months of the assignment we weren't considered Peace Corps members. The "in country" training did not even count towards the two years of volunteer service. I am sure the others were doing the same thing I was in my head by calculating just how old I was going to be and when we would be getting out.

Another thing that I must have missed some where in the literature was that we would have to meet a certain proficiency of the language within those first three months. An independent embassy member would then test us, and if we could not make that proficiency, we would be flown back to the United States with a handshake and a kiss good bye. That was a strong incentive because I was sure no one wanted to be the failure flown back.

Language was not my best subject in college and I managed to get into a degree program that did not require a second language for graduation. I could not bear the thought and embarrassment I would feel in being sent back.

The next shock was the profile of the people that were with me. We had one guy who actually brought a surfboard with him saying that he heard Central America had some "awesome" waves.

There was a girl who brought a hair dryer, electric fan and toaster and she was scheduled for a jungle assignment like mine. I had some limited experience seeing poverty first hand in Egypt and Turkey but most of these pre-volunteers had never even been out of the United States.

I started to wonder if I was the only one with thoughts that poverty meant no running water, no electricity and not the best of food.

I would just kind of grin and bear the comments and would think back to the day in my University of Texas geography class when one of the girls sitting next to me leaned over and asked me where in the U.S. New York City was located. Therefore, I reasoned that why would I think these young people should know any better about what they were in for?

By the same token I think the others thought I was weird because of my jungle hammock, although the boots they wrote off as me having just come from Texas.

I would become every one's best friend by day three because almost all of them were over the weight allowance and I had plenty to share.

I met another interesting fellow who was a biologist and was planning on teaching fishery to the Nicaraguans, in addition to setting up his own fishing business. He figured land, labor and fish stock would be real cheap to acquire and in no time flat he could be in business.

I remember asking him if he could purchase land while being a volunteer and he commented back that he would just have to find a Nicaraguan partner and put it in his name. I'm sure he didn't let Peace Corps in on that idea during the screening process.

The elderly lady of the group was, or seemed to be, the most concerned about going because her son worked in the embassy and this was a chance to be near him and her grandchildren. Only she planned on using her own money to supplement her living style while there. Again this was something I was sure the Peace Corps was not aware of and would not encourage or condone.

Even though Peace Corps was open to all ages and ethic backgrounds, I would encounter only a very few elderly, married, and only one Hispanic.

Two other interesting members of the group were very rugged looking, and seemed to fit my Peace Corps perception. Both were members of the Sierra Club, avid backpackers, and talked the talk of wanting to help the natives. They seemed to click real well together and almost looked like a couple prior to the end of staging.

* * * *

The staging was well organized, constructed and presented. I thought it might have been designed to give any one who wanted it, a last chance to ditch and run with dignity.

Peace Corps stressed that while it was a volunteer assignment, they wanted a sincere and dedicated commitment to their goal. They did not want people thinking it was a paid vacation or student excursion we were going on.

We were given a half day of free time prior to our next day departure and I convinced my room mate to go with me to a serpent zoological park. Most of the pre-volunteers headed to the bar or their rooms to catch up on sleep but for me this was just another once-in-a-lifetime event to see asps, cobras and rattlesnakes being milked for their venom.

My roommate wasn't sure why he went along but I suppose it was for the same reason that people go to auto races, not to see the race as much as to see if there is a five car pile up in front of them.

I think he felt it was exciting to see these guys handling these venomous snakes and wondering if someone was going to get bitten. I started wondering what we might run into down in Nicaragua and I couldn't help but smile looking down at our feet, me in boots and him in sneakers. I was sure I had chosen wisely.

* * * *

We were informed on the day of departure, April 4th 1977, that because of a Nicaraguan holiday, we would be staying with some volunteers assigned in the capital region. Then, on the next day, would be going up into the mountains to where our host families and the training center were located.

The training site was located in Jenotepe, which was a small town up a winding road from the capital and into the mountainous area where coffee and tobacco is grown. The temperature there would drop a good ten degrees making it much more pleasant than the hot capital area and much more scenic.

Each volunteer is assigned to live with a host country family that doesn't speak English. This was done to facilitate more conversational Spanish time during the training period. This would also prevent the volunteers from segregating themselves in country to be around other volunteers or English-speaking groups.

Chapter

3

Quality Family Time

The first day in Nicaragua was rather uneventful as we were worn out from the excitement of the staging the previous couple of days. While it was not a long flight, we were tired from all the time spent in the airports because of all the baggage and the fact that we were a relatively large group.

So after loading too many people and bags on one very small bus, we went off to different volunteers' homes to spend our first night in-country. Three others and I stayed with a couple that was living together. They decided the best way to prepare us for our assignment was to feed us the "typical" Nicaraguan meal, which consisted of nothing more than beans and rice mixed together. I am relatively sure it was in the back of the minds of the other pre-volunteers that maybe this was just a fast, easy and cheap way to feed us. We would gladly have paid for their meal as well had they just taken us to a restaurant. It was comical, to me, that volunteers living in the capital area and having access to all the amenities wanted to show us how they "rough" it.

The treat for dessert was fried platinos, which was nothing more to me than a fried, green banana. I really didn't care much for the meal and did not relish the idea of everyone being in tight quarters for the night having just downed a big bowl of beans. Besides, I ate all I could at the airport and on the plane. Regardless of what most people say, airplane food can be your best friend when deadheading to a third world country.

Boy was I glad that night to have that jungle hammock because there was a shortage of sleeping room in the Inn. For those that don't know what a jungle hammock is, it's a sleeping bag with ropes that are suspended between two trees. You just get in, zip up, and sleep the night away swinging in the breeze. I was, perhaps, the most comfortable that night.

* * * *

The next morning, which was a Sunday, the bus took us around and dropped each of us off at the home of our host family. The look on most of the volunteer's faces was one of fear, dread, and a hope that their house was not next. It was somewhat like having a fear of sky diving and waiting your turn to jump. Finally my turn arrived and there was not much of an introduction, not that there could be, because the family didn't speak a word of English, and I couldn't say more in Spanish than the Ten Little Indians.

The bus driver tossed my belongings on the stoop and off went the bus. It was almost like the first day of school. I didn't know whether to be excited or sit down and cry!

The mother and father greeted me and showed me my room, which was no bigger than some Americans' bathrooms. I had a little dresser and night table next to my single bed. I unpacked in about three minutes and put my only semi-precious belonging, a small cassette radio, on the nightstand and off I went to be hospitable and explore the house.

The house was in a u-shape with the typical inner courtyard where the eating table was. One apparently ate outdoors and I wondered right off what we were going to do if it rained. I figured they must have a back up plan; after all, they had been living there quite awhile. All in all, I did think it was nice to be able to look at the stars while eating.

The main living room, or "sala" as it is known in Spanish, was in an open area as well. The sala had a sofa, two chairs, a standing lamp and a TV that looked like a hold over from the early sixties.

Most rooms with the exception of the bedrooms and bathrooms are open to the courtyard to remain cool throughout the tropical year since there is no air conditioning.

There was a small bathroom just outside my room, which was for my use. The shower and the toilet shared the same space. You could shower while you sat! Now, I'm not one of those men who like to sit on the throne and read, but at the end of a particularly hot tropical day, it was good to sit and relax while the cold water hit you on the head.

I was quick to notice that some other creatures also liked my bathroom. A chill went up my spine looking at the webs on the ceiling; I guess they needed the spiders to keep the rest of the crawlers at bay. And I do mean crawlers with lots of legs! There were these things that looked like centipedes. I'm a firm believer that nothing, insect or mammal, needs more than four legs. It was disgusting to see so many legs on one creature all moving at the same time!

* * * *

The floors of the house were tile. We had running water and electricity, so altogether it was an average, middle class family home. They even had a TV, which they went back to watching as they eyed me looking around.

When the two daughters around the ages of fifteen and seventeen arrived, I was introduced. I got the feeling from the father that it was 'hands off' or I would find myself shark bait in the Atlantic Ocean. Actually, he would have only had to cart me over to Lake Managua. The lake was about thirty kilometers away, and Nicaragua has the only fresh water shark in the world, which evolved when Lake Managua was gradually closed off from the ocean.

The introduction had a whole lot of Spanish words for "this is Kirk" and "this is Rosa". I noticed right away from the older daughter's voice and words with her father, that trouble was just a blink away. I got the look from her that said,"Oh boy, fresh meat".

The mother decided to break the mood by motioning me over to the table to eat. I had to admit that I was as hungry as a horse, and I had been known to out eat my football friends in college, but nothing prepared me for this meal.

I thought it odd that no one else sat down to eat but figured it was close to eight o'clock and maybe they had already eaten. The meal was a non-stop ordeal and in order to not offend anyone, I ate every thing she dished at me until finally I thought I would toss. She broke my spirit at last. I cried "uncle" and that was the end of the food conveyer.

I waddled over and sat on the sofa to watch some TV with the parents. I was happy to see "Little House on the Prairie" with Michael Landon, in Spanish. The set was black and white but was the main entertainment for the family.

I thought I would take a run at speaking something in Spanish so I put together a couple of words I did know, which were "casa", meaning house and "chico" meaning little. So I pointed at the TV and said, "casa chico, casa chico". The mother and father got this worried look on their faces, and the next thing I know, there's a dialog going on between them for which I'm at a total loss.

In a mad dash the mother runs off and returns with a roll of toilet paper and hands it to me. It didn't take a rocket scientist to piece that one together. I refrained from coming up with any more words at that moment, accepted the roll, and went off to my bedroom. I figured with my speaking capability, at that point, I could get into more trouble trying to use what little Spanish I did know than it was worth.

* * * *

That first night I was very tired, and the bed was as lumpy as a sack full of rocks. Had the Princess in the classic fairy tale "Princess and the Pea" been in my bed that night, she would have been dead by morning, but I had my radio and turned off the lights.

Now, with the exception of a few small screened windows at the top of one wall facing the courtyard, it was pitch black in that room, just the way I like a bedroom. About an hour into the night I felt something hit the bed. I sat up and saw something crawling. I pulled the light chain, and to my horror, it was what looked like the biggest cockroach on the planet. I grabbed my shoe to hit it and it flew off.

Hey, no cockroach I ever saw could fly, at least not that I was aware of! I whacked it against the wall and felt that feeling you have in your stomach as it made that mushy crunching sound.

The next thing I knew the father was knocking on my door. He stood there in boxer shorts and tee shirt, and in Spanish, probably wanted to know if every thing was all right. I stuck my head around the door, not wanting to show off my underwear, and motioned as best I could that every thing couldn't be better.

We reached an unspoken agreement not to let it happen again. I was a bit angered by this short, dumpy, bald guy talking to me in Spanish like I understood every word and in a tone like he was giving me orders.

Not wanting to be the ugly American I apologized as best I could, figuring I could just as well have been smiling while saying, "Kiss my butt and you deal with these bird size flying rodents!"

The father, who ruled over three women, his wife and two daughters, as macho man would need to think again before dealing with me. I was born with my mother's fighting instinct. As a result of his personality and mine, neither he nor I would care for each other over the training period. He reminded me of some of those men who suffer from short-man syndrome and need to prove themselves.

I would find out later that Peace Corps played no part in the screening or picking of these families and that the families did not do this out of any reason other than economical gain. The company that Peace Corps contracted with to do the training selected the families.

Maybe in retrospect, he wanted to make sure his daughter wasn't in there with me. Not that I considered myself some kind of ladies' man, but as most guys could probably tell, his older daughter was not big on morals.

That would not be the last time the flying cockroaches wanted to walk on me at night. Unfortunately I lost my radio within the first week trying to beat them back with anything I could throw at them.

It was hard to get to sleep at night thinking of their flat bodies and twitching antenna scouting me out like I was some kind of potential mega meal. I came to like spiders, for the first time in my life, so long as they stayed a respectable size.

* * * *

Now, most Americans have been introduced, saturated and brainwashed about Spanish people, their traditions and food as it applies to Mexico.

I found that the people in Nicaragua did not even know what a taco or burrito was, much less anything about sombreros or siestas. I would learn that the Latin culture, even in neighboring countries like Costa Rica, El Salvador, Guatemala and Honduras, are completely different from Mexico and in many cases with each other.

Chapter

4

The Training

By morning, my stomach was still hurting from all the food I had eaten the night before. I thought, offend or not, there was no way I could stuff that much down again. I was determined I was going to turn down food or need a wheel chair by the end of training if I didn't act fast. The bus came by to pick me up that first morning and standing there waiting made me feel like an elementary schooler except no lunch pail.

I was never so glad to be going somewhere, as I was that first day. I was actually looking forward to seeing the other volunteers. We arrived at the school and divided up into classes of about six to a group.

They needed to keep the groups small to get as much one-on-one as they could with the language to get us up to speed as fast as possible with communication skills. We had the normal welcoming from the Peace Corps in-country administration and training staff.

This was where the Nicaraguan Peace Corps Director laid out the rules for what behavior he would or would not accept. The Peace Corps had an image to protect so they would not tolerate inappropriate actions or behavior on the part of the volunteers and they would return you to the U.S. if you did not comply. It was also a time for re-enforcement of our commitment.

We were asked to comment on how things went the first day with our family. Almost every one had no comment or just said, "Fine", maybe because of the prior speeches they were intimidated, but when it got to good old honest me, I decided to approach the topic of eating and not wanting to offend my host family by turning down food.

Little did I know that by offering my feelings on the first day, those statements would be carried immediately back to the family in order to rectify any uncomfortable situation the volunteer may have had.

To my amazement, I would be told at the end of the day that the center had indeed sent someone to my family's house to address the issue of mealtime.

One of the center staff was laughing so hard that she could barely tell me what happened. It seemed that she told my family that I did not want to offend them but could not eat that much food.

What was so funny to her became an embarrassment to me. Imagine how I felt finding out I had consumed the entire meal of the entire family that night. They were worried over the perceived cost of feeding me for an extended length of time. I couldn't bear the thought of going home to face them, and the other volunteers thought it was a hoot!

* * * *

I learned that I could walk to the center and used the walking as a time to think and meditate. This was something I would do often during my training period to explore the town and practice my Spanish on the unprepared natives. Furthermore I could escape the family time and potential run in with the father of the family.

The first two weeks were indeed intense with not only Spanish but also lessons in history, geography, and culture.

I was worried from the beginning because every one seemed to be picking up the language faster than I was and I had that fearful thought of being the only one not swearing in at the embassy in just a couple of months.

At the beginning of week three the volunteers started bailing out and heading back to the United States. Each day, from then on, I wondered who would be next. My staging roommate, surfer dude and electric lady were some of the first to go.

The rough and tough girl that was going to the coast showed up one day in my class. The training program would rotate the volunteers around to keep the fast paced ones together and the slower ones in a more hands on class.

I am not sure but I would venture to say I was part of the group of drooling slowpokes. Anyway, to our delight, she showed up in our class with a sleeveless blouse and was against wearing a bra. Because she was good looking, the guys just couldn't help trying to get a peek, me included. What I wasn't ready for was the underarm hair that was longer than mine! That was only half of it because she had been masking the fact that she used no deodorant.

By the third day, three of us got together to draw straws on who had to tell her that we couldn't bear the smell any more and it was hard to concentrate on the training each time a breeze came through the window.

Thank God I was not short straw because she was hard as nails and a "get in your face" type of person. She insisted that deodorant was unhealthy and she wasn't about to use it. We asked that she not raise her hand or stretch her arms out during the breaks which may have sounded rude but human body odors in a tropical climate can nearly kill. Even the teacher applauded our mission. We were giving the locals a whole new meaning of "stinky American". She did, however, not wear any more sleeveless blouses, much to our joy.

* * * *

On the third weekend I talked another volunteer into going with me to look at a live volcano, something I had always wanted to do. While in college in Munich, Germany, I had tried to get someone to go to Italy with me to see one live and erupting, but no takers, not even anyone from the geology department.

On any bus ride you could see just about everything from chickens on board to pigs on top. On the way to the volcano site, the other volunteer and I went towards the back of the bus and sat down across from what I would say was one of the most attractive women I have ever seen.

In her arms was an infant, which meant no chance of getting to know her. We just kind of watched out the window and when not looking obvious, would glance over at her.

I am not sure how it happened, but at the same time, both the other volunteer and I glanced over and watched as she unbuttoned her blouse and removed her breast and popped the nipple in the baby's mouth. My fellow volunteer and I looked on this with amazement. We chatted about that once we got off the bus. Both of us had the same opinion that it was one of the most beautiful things we had ever seen. It was as natural and elegant as any thing I had witnessed in terms of human nature.

Back to the volcano. It was off limits per instructions of the Peace Corps, but to see a live volcano was a once in a lifetime experience. Up the mountain we went with insufficient water and moving like the thing was going to disappear if we didn't get there soon.

By the time we got to the rim we were dehydrated and almost unconscious from the sulfur fumes. The sulfur gas was what told us we were close, but what we were not prepared for was that we were on a ledge, which was a shear drop off of about 300 yards. It was one of the most incredible sites I have ever seen and the lava was shooting up two to three hundred feet in the air.

When we noticed that the ledge we were on turned in under us, we realized just how much danger we were in and took it nice and slow backing up. We must have looked like crawling turtles while listening for any sign that the ledge was giving way under our weight. By the time we got back down it was evening and we were nearly dizzy from thirst.

* * * *

Into the forth week the elder daughter of my host family, together with her sister, started plotting on how to use the gringo to their advantage. Like the naive person I could be, I fell right into their plans. I was invited to a party with them. The only way the father would allow them to stay out beyond eleven was with me in tow.

I was abandoned within five minutes of arrival at the party. Because my Spanish was still rather limited, the male participants at the party were constantly goofing on me, or so I was convinced because they would say, "the gringo this or that" and then laugh.

I believe it was a macho put down thing because many of the girls were thinking, "Oh boy, a new toy!" and wanted to talk to me. I could tell by their attention it was more than just casual talk they were trying to make.

At about one o'clock in the morning the younger daughter tracked me down and was in a panic because the older one had hooked up with someone and disappeared. The problem was, the guy had taken her back to his house and little sister didn't know where he lived.

We waited until around two o'clock but she never showed up. We knew we were in trouble because it was way beyond the time we should have been back. So the younger one and I went home.

I remember walking through the front door and the father was all over us, shouting at me and the younger one in Spanish. I could figure out from the conversation that the younger one felt kind of bad for me and stuck up for me.

I just looked worried, kind of lifted my shoulders and hands every now and then to show that if he wanted to lop off my head I wouldn't resist. He grabbed a razor strap and flew out the door. I ran for my room and hoped I could get out of this family living as soon as possible.

* * * *

The next day at school I asked if I could get a key to the building so I could use the blackboard to help me in the conjugating of verbs and sentence writing in Spanish. The head of the center allowed me to have one. This also gave me the opportunity to get away from the family living situation.

By the start of the fifth week Peace Corps was upset because we had lost over half the group due to volunteers returning home. It was one of the worst records to date for returns.

One of the reasons for so many returns had to do with the conditions. Malaria pills were a requirement and there was a big debate over them. Some of the volunteers said that the benefits did not outweigh the side effects and would not take them. Peace Corps took the position that if you were caught not taking them, your assignment would be terminated.

My feeling was that whatever the side effects were couldn't be nearly as bad as what I had read about malaria. I took my pill each day without a second thought. It was like taking birth control pills though; you had to take it everyday or the consequences were with you for life! Besides, I knew I was getting a jungle assignment and was a prime candidate for exposure.

Another issue had to do with the families they were living with. Many of them had problems with the over bearing nature of the traditional Nicaraguan head of household. In many ways, most volunteers felt they weren't treated well or very kindly.

It would seem that a number of host families had agreed to sponsor volunteers purely for the extra income rather than any humanitarian reasons. They certainly didn't go out of their way to make welcome those that had come to help them. I was included in that group. During my entire stay at their house I never once felt welcome.

Food might have been another factor that played a role in the drop out rate because you would always be hearing the trainees talking about exchanging body parts for a cheese burger, pizza and other foods they were use to. It seemed every chance they got they went to the places that catered to more American cuisine.

* * * *

I had adjusted to the cockroaches crawling around at night and didn't hear the buzzing noise of their wings any more. From then on I made sure to sleep with the covers over my mouth. I had heard that the average person swallows eight insects while sleeping in a lifetime and I didn't want the Guinness world record!

Hell, by this time I had even given up on picking the flying insects out of my meals at night unless they were flies. Just scoop and eat while not looking.

I think each Nicaraguan flying insect went through Kamikaze training and were taught to dive bomb on the soft or moist foods first and it never failed they would go for the few things I liked the best. After having a few kerplunk in my cokes I learned real fast to drink only from a bottle and not a glass because it gave them a harder target to shoot at. Not only that, but certain bugs in a coke is like alka-seltzer in water, there one minute and seem to be gone the next with the exception of a wing or two.

I am not even sure why the family had screens on the kitchen windows because the mother kept the door open all day long and I think they actually trapped more flies in than keeping them out.

I had, by now, even come to the point of discovering my favorite food, which was fried cheese.

This cheese was so salty you would swear you were a deer in the woods at the salt lick. They would take slabs of it and pan fry it until it was golden brown.

* * * *

Most of these weeks, I was staying late at the center using the blackboard and arriving home way past dinnertime. One night I came home and saw the mother spraying "El Tigre", which means 'the tiger' and is an insect spray, above my food to keep the flies away. A few had dropped dead in my food, which she proceeded to pick out.

I really didn't think much of it at the time, but at about one in the morning I was in a cold sweat and vomiting what I thought were my lungs out. I thought I was going to die just from the heaving.

I truly learned the meaning of hugging the bowl, as I could not get up off of all fours because of the intensity and fatigue. I immediately knew why El Tigre kills every thing that moves just short of me. I told the mother the next morning that she needed to cover my food, not spray it.

* * * *

An odd thing happened around week seven when a new volunteer arrived. He was very Latin looking and spoke Spanish as a native. This puzzled the few of us left but we were told he was sent to get our numbers up and that he joined, already knowing the language. I had not paid much attention to the rumors of the anti-government guerilla movement in the North. I had, however, overheard some of the in-country training staff talk about the fact that, for political reasons, this would be the last training program. Apparently, it would be done by another firm next go round because of their political beliefs.

The real odd thing came on Sunday when I went down to the center to use the blackboard with my key in hand. Upon entering the building, I had to pass the main administration office, to get to the room I liked to use best.

The door was open, and sitting there going over our personnel files, was the new volunteer. Not only did he not have a key to the building, but only the director had a key to the administration office, and the file cabinet was under lock and key as well, something I would ask about later in the week.

To distract my attention, the volunteer said, "Man you wouldn't believe what they have written about you, would you like to see?" I said no, I just needed to study on the blackboard and went to the room with what I remember to be a real uneasy feeling about this guy.

He seemed psychopathic to me and having worked these last years with different disorders and studied about them, I thought it best I not intrude. He left me alone as well.

Later I would find out that his assignment was as a hospital administrator, which would give him free and understandable travel throughout the country. One of the other Peace Corps volunteers, who had the same role, was convinced that not only did the guy not know anything about hospital administration, or very little, but his background of schooling didn't make any sense for this profession either.

A question in my mind, in later years was, if this guy was a Central Intelligence Agency (C.I.A.) operative who had free access to the entire northern region, blended in as Latin, and spoke perfect Spanish, why was he concerned with Peace Corps volunteers?

* * * *

By the last week, I was a nervous wreck, worried about making the language requirement. The day came to step into the room with the embassy tester, and I did just fine. All the weeks of blackboard time paid off and I went slow and spoke softly, measuring each sentence and trying to use the right verb in its right tense. What throws a lot of Americans off trying to learn the language is all the different variations of the tenses and the way the sentence structure is laid out. Every thing seemed backwards to me. Where I would say the "red wagon" they would say the "wagon red". It was a constant process of thinking before you spoke.

I worried as I saw her writing things down, but when the end came, she said the only thing I needed to do was speak faster. I told her I went slow because I didn't want to get it wrong and I was nervous almost to the point of peeing in my pants. She laughed and said she understood.

On the last day of the training period, June 24th 1977, I proudly raised my right hand along with the other two volunteers and pledged my allegiance.   I was now an official Peace Corps Volunteer.   I was ready to start my two years of service.

5

The Work Site

Arriving in Condega which was a northern pueblo of Nicaragua, per Peace Corps instructions, I immediately checked in with the Nicaraguan national guard. I explained who I was and why I was there which was required by the National Guard to keep tabs on the locals. The National Guard only maintained a small checkpoint at the entrance to the pueblo, which was manned by two guards. This allowed the government to keep a presence in the more remote areas.

I then proceeded to get a room at the local hotel, if you want to call it that. If I had owned a pet it could have left when it wanted to under the door. No windows, a single bed, one small broken dresser, and a 25-watt light bulb hanging from the ceiling. Geez! What was it about the fact that whenever I got electricity it was from no more than a 25 watt bulb!   I had flashbacks of my family and the webs on the ceiling!

I got to share the bathroom with around eight other guests at the time. The shower was a vintage bathtub from, I would say, the 1920s and a curtain ring suspended above it which made a circle around the inside of the tub.   Likewise, the faucet was not at the end of the tub, but dead center above and delivered barely enough water pressure to wet your face, let alone the rest of your body. I had had people sneeze on me with more force and moisture! It was so small in circumference that anyone, of any size, might find the "moldy plastic death shroud" clinging to their bodies if they dared to move inside the shower area.

Still I didn't care; I threw my things on the bed and headed out the door to see my pueblo. It looked like a western because all the roads were dirt and there were hitching posts in front of the stores where horses were tied up.

* * * *

I met the other volunteer, David, who was also at this site. He had already been there a year and worked for the Agriculture Department whereas I would be working for the Ministry of Health.

My job was to work with a team of five Nicaraguan civil engineer types going out into the surrounding mountains to provide wells for potable water, latrines, and finding out which children needed vaccinations. I had never done any of these things before, nor been trained to do them, so I figured it would take about a days worth of on the job training.

This job was why the Peace Corps nurse kept coming to the training center, and at the end, I was the only one getting it in my end. I was going into a 100 percent malaria and typhoid zone, so I got extra shots and doubles on others.

* * * *

During the first couple of weeks we went out daily in four-wheel jeeps. Our job was to dig wells so the campesinos could drink clean water instead of from the streams where the cattle were drinking, wading and every other foul thing. We then built outhouses to avoid using the streams the way the animals did. The reason for the jeeps was to get the cement needed for the wells, and the lumber and tin needed for the outhouses to the sites. We took on the closest sites first.

I am not sure whom the brain surgeon was that thought up the idea of making the outhouses out of aluminum. In a tropical climate you would cook just putting them up, let alone sitting in one and getting down to business! It didn't take long for the campesinos to complain and head back to the refreshing stream instead.

* * * *

My other objective during the first two weeks was to find one of the poorest families in town and cut a deal to pay for a room in cash and labor. I decided that if I did that, I could make a change in their lives and not have it look like gratuities.

I found my family quick. They had eight kids, a house roughly twelve feet by twelve with the living area, two small rooms, a bedroom where the family slept like hamsters and a storage room.

Mine was the storage room, which was roughly three feet across and seven feet long, just enough room for my scissor bed. A scissor bed is like a cot, only when you fold it open, it sits about four feet off the ground so you hop in it instead of climbing in. The reason for the height was to keep the crawlers off of you at night, and believe me, it was one of my first purchases.

It did not seem practical for me to rent from the family and then go outside and hang my sleeping hammock in the back yard so my use of this treasure was short lived.

Anyway, the house had dirt floors, no running water, an outhouse about thirty feet back, chickens and pigs indoors with us, and a see-through curtain for my door. Two of the children had tested positive for TB, but all in all, every one was fairly healthy so I struck my deal and it was accepted.

The first night the kids would pull the curtain back and laugh like crazy while pointing at me in my underwear because, to them, this was entertainment where little existed.

I guess a tall gringo in his underwear is well worth a good laugh when nothing much else goes on. The next morning, as I stepped in pig droppings, I insisted that no more chickens or pigs should be allowed in the house! I could tell that that was not going to happen. They were used to dodging the poop but I wasn't. I even thought about wearing my boots to bed.

I paid the father and, immediately after handing him the cash, he decided he was going to tell me what labor to do. I stopped him right there and said, "Look, I am putting a cement and tile floor in the house as my first labor". His eyes got as big as saucers and his grin went from ear to ear.

I immediately had a flash of wondering what this was going to cost me. I quickly put that out of my mind because of the difference it would make for his children and the sanitation of his home and what was, for the time being, my home too!

I got a hold of another volunteer in a nearby city that had use of a jeep and I went and got the cement and tiles the next day. When we showed up to drop off the cement and tile at the house, the other volunteer said to me, "Are you kidding? You're living here?"

It took only two days to get the floor in and the father ended up doing most of the labor but what a happy man he was. The nice thing was that the family was so proud of the floor they no longer wanted the chickens and pigs inside; I considered it a mission accomplished.

* * * *

Meanwhile, back at work, we kept venturing further out. Now, it was drive in with the jeeps as far as we could, then strap the wood, tin, and cement on mules and get on our horses and go. It was a good thing I did as much horseback riding as I had in Texas, but those first days my rump and other unmentionables still hurt.

There was something about my Nicaraguan horses though. They seemed to always want to stop in the streams and drink themselves silly.

After that, I would never again give any weight to the phrase "you can lead a horse to water but you can not make him drink". No matter how much I kicked they got as stubborn as could be. Inevitably one of the others would have to turn around, ride back and grab my horse's reins. I guess I just didn't have the heart to spur them, which I never did, and they were trained to the spurs.

I had a canteen that I took with me and would put the iodine tablets in the water to help stop the possible spread of typhoid or other infectious diseases. It tasted like rusty water and looked like rusty water so, in addition, I started taking with me bottles of Coke strapped to my belt and all the others thought I was nuts. I figured if I was going to have to drink something brown it might as well taste good. Hot coke tasted better than that water any day, even though it increased my thirst level in the hot climate.

Word got out among the campesinos that when the gringo got to their location if they had coke they could sell it to him for quite a profit. I didn't mind paying through the nose because I would be so thirsty I would give my left big toe nail for it. Besides I knew they needed the money and they went to all the trouble to get it and have it available and now I no longer needed to strap it to my belt.

* * * *

Well into month four at the site, I was getting fairly well adapted, except for working conditions. Most of our wells and latrine building was getting further out and the insects were crawling up my legs and doing a number on me.

I would tie my pant legs down, but the most disgusting thing was the riding through clouds of gnat like insects, which would fly in our eyes, ears, and mouth if we opened it. The buggers would fly up my nose, cause me to open my mouth, and in they would go until I would gag, and spit them out.

One of my most exasperating days came when we had finished a deep and hard to construct well and the water sample had come back clean.

We proceeded to commend the campesinos on a job well done. One of them, standing next to the well, leaning on his shovel, hocked up a big luggie and spit it down the well.

I almost fell down I was so upset; he didn't think any thing was wrong. I explained we were going to have to chlorinate the well and resample it again before they could drink from it. What a bummer.

* * * *

I decided it was time to do my next major improvement for the family. I had talked to the other volunteer, David, who was the agriculturalist, about what kinds of vegetables grew in the region that I could try growing behind the house.   He came over to where I was living, looked at me, and said something to the effect that he knew campesinos that had it better.   I explained that I wanted to increase the food supply to the family, and vary the types, while showing that we could do it at little or no expense.   The family would then be able to continue on from there.

David helped me get all the seeds I needed via the Peace Corps, which included about three types of melons, carrots, cabbage, and a whole slew of others.   I bought pots and set up a giant table out back.   I had over two hundred seedlings growing by week three.   I babied those plants like they were my children.   By the time they were ready for transplant into the huge garden I had ready, tilled with fertilizers and such, I knew that this was going to be a vast improvement.

That night I went to sleep and the next morning, when I was going to do the transplanting, I came outside to see nothing but stems everywhere I looked. All of my plants had been eaten by the chickens which the neighbors had let loose.

I was devastated.   All those hours and now I had to start over again.   I went out and bought about twelve yards of chicken wire and started over determined that this was going to succeed.

The effort did not take as long on the second go round because I only had to reseed the pots, water, and wait.   About one month into it we had melons and carrots and eggplant and all sorts of things popping up to where the mother really started to get excited and take an interest. She was starting to tend the garden full time which was what I had hoped for but what I was to find out was that instead of cooking them she was selling them. I am not sure I was changing the kid's diets because, with the exception of some of the melon, she was selling it all.

While I felt it was good the mother now had a means of helping out economically, I was not satisfied I was accomplishing my goal. I figured the problem must be that she didn't know how to prepare the variety of food in any other than the customary way she was taught so I would need to show her. The problem was, I was clueless on how to cook or prepare anything myself. I had never made any thing with eggplant or squash, nor did I know how to peel a green bean. After looking at the wood-burning stove I decided I better come up with a different plan.

In no time flat I was inspired by looking at the chicken wire and decided food would still be the mission but raising chickens for the meat and eggs was going to be the way. I remembered seeing a stove some volunteer had made out of a five gallon cooking oil container and using the sun so I figured with a few modifications I could easily invent an incubator for the eggs. I decided I had my next family project all mapped out in my head.

* * * *

One day, while walking by some new construction that was going on in the pueblo, something I saw sparked my interest. The cement wall that had been constructed three days previously had a couple of construction guys chiseling a square out of one side.

I couldn't help but stop and ask what they were doing. They thought I was stupid for asking because it was a window.   For the next four days I watched them chisel this crude square in the side of the wall.   I made a mental note to not involve them in any thing I might do in the future.

Because the Somosa family not only ran the country, but also owned the cement factories in the country, and had a monopoly on the government contracts. Half of the things in the country were made out of cement. That was the first time I had ever seen a cement telephone pole.

Chapter

6

Just Dying For A Vacation

One night, while at my adopted home sitting in one of the rocking chairs talking with some of the kids, the mother brought the kids and me a glass of milk which I accepted and drank down. I asked what it was and was told fresh cow's milk with sugar added. This was a real treat for the kids and I figured since it had been heated, no problem.

I am not sure if it was the milk or something else I had consumed along the way of my daily life in the pueblo, but a time bomb was about to go off in my stomach that would prove nearly fatal to me!

When I first started my assignment, I tried to be conscientious about what I ate, how it was prepared and where, but as the weeks rolled into months, it was easy to let down my guard and try more things. The food supply in Nicaragua was so limited that one could count the variety of dishes on two hands and still come up with fingers left over. Out of boredom I would occasionally try something different to make eating less of a necessity, and more of the joy it used to be.

I had been taking most of my meals at one of the two eating holes in town and had to trust that what was coming out was clean.

I did not have either the facilities or the means to be cooking my own food. That may sound crazy but the stove was an old wood burner, and there was no refrigeration. This, on top of the fact that no matter where I stocked dry goods, they needed super sealing to prevent intrusion by crawlers.

It may have been possible for volunteers assigned in the cities but for us out in the sticks, well, we just had to get our food where we could.

I am not sure if it's mind over matter or the other way around, but my system became somewhat trained to know what it could tolerate and what it couldn't. Generally, after a few bites of something, I had a sixth sense for what would or wouldn't sit well. I think elderly people can identify with this understanding.

After drinking the milk and retiring for the night, I could sense something was wrong. At about two in the morning, I had the familiar, but dreaded gastrointestinal distress, and it's a pain to get up and hike out to the outhouse. I immediately knew I was in trouble so started the trek to the old smelly house. I made it just in time and, like Moby Dick, blew from both ends at the same time. Within minutes, I was in a cold sweat from the abdominal cramps and was ready to pass out. As I sat there, I knew things were getting worse and I wanted to head back to the room and get to the trusted Peace Corps medical kit.

Now, one of the most important items a newly sworn in Peace Corps member gets prior to deployment is his medical kit. This kit has some nice items in it and the one most valuable was a bottle of lomatil, which can stop diarrhea in minutes.

Trying to get from the outhouse back to my room became a monumental task. I kept passing out every few feet and falling on the ground, coming to and then repeating the process.

Once I fell into the barbed wire fence, which separated the neighbor's property, and I could feel it ripping my skin on the slide down, which tore me up and hurt like the dickens. I could relate to why that wire is used to contain prisoners.

I could hear the pigs getting closer and started thinking I better not pass out again or these buggers are going to make a meal of me. I remembered the story of the campesina who went to bed with her baby. Sometime during the night the baby fell out of bed and by morning had been nearly consumed.

I could just imagine Peace Corps telling my folks, "Sorry, your son was eaten by pigs in Nicaragua". "Serving" in the Peace Corps shouldn't mean so literally.

I did make it back to the room after repeated trips back to the outhouse, and then forward again, just as it was getting light outside. The Nicaraguan women were almost always up around four or five in the morning to pat out the tortillas for the day. I would have been the talk of the town caught coming from the outhouse in just my underwear and boots! My incentive to make it back was more out of pride rather than fear.

Once in my room, I downed as many lomatil as I thought safe, dressed, and headed for the bus stop as fast as I could go. I knew I needed to get to a hospital, so I boarded the bus and headed to the next city hoping that I could control myself until I reached safe haven.

As I rode in the bus I passed out and woke up in the capital, which was just as well. I got over to the hotel that the volunteers used, and was pleased to see one of the volunteer nurses there.

I explained what I drank, and what followed, and she felt it might be a form of food poisoning, which would pass. Comforted, I got a room and the rest of the day was uneventful with the exception of fatigue.

Later that night, I was having a repeat episode of earlier, only this time, worse. I started to hallucinate and see creatures coming out from the walls like in a bad 3D movie. I knew they weren't real but man that was weird.

I remember thinking that if this is what a druggie sees on a bad trip, who would want to repeat that same excursion again. The nurse got to me and called the administration of Peace Corps. She told them what bad shape I was in and that I needed a doctor ASAP.

I had not paid too much attention to the political climate and there were a lot of demonstrations and shooting in the streets that night. Rather than have me get out of bed, Peace Corps had the support doctor come to me. I had to give credit to that Nicaraguan doctor because he shot straight from the hip and told it like he saw it.

He said if I didn't get more fluids in me by morning, I might be dead. Maybe his bedside manner was a little off because he did not like coming to the hotel under the circumstances, but he put me into action. The nurse got me about four liters of Coke while I sat on the throne and drank, heaved, and "hershied" myself silly.

The bathroom was small, which was great, because as I would get ready to pass out, I could fall against the door or lean forward and hang on to the sink. All in all, it was a horrifying night, unpleasant beyond my wildest dreams, and infinitely embarrassing.

I would venture to guess that the hotel would have loved to have boarded up the bathroom for whatever length of time it takes to be free of radioactive material.

The next day, Peace Corps got me proper medical attention. They diagnosed me as having a parasitic condition in advanced stages and harvesting the intestinal walls to the point of internal bleeding. One thing you have to give Peace Corps credit for is taking care of their volunteers.

I was put in a convent with some nuns who babied and pampered me. While there I went through the stages of taking the medication that nearly "kills while trying to cure" the problem.

The week I spent there was the best and a most needed vacation. After I got past this medical problem, Peace Corps insisted that I better my living conditions.   Although they felt my intentions were admirable, I was to change, or they would send me back home.

* * * *

I spent some time in the Peace Corps library just prior to returning, leafing through the medical journals and nursing magazines and got a terrific idea. I knew the statistics showed the infant mortality rate in the northern region to be extreme and that only about 40% have a chance of living past three years of age.

I knew that no child, much less a baby should have to go through what I just had, but the cold reality was they did. Getting the fluids in order to get your electrolytes up becomes essential for survival. I, at least, had the electrolyte packets from my Peace Corps medical kit.

What the Peace Corps nurse told me is that not only do the campesinas not have electrolyte packets but also they usually react in the opposite way necessary. They think that to stop fluids from coming out, they had to stop them from going in. Consequently, it was often dehydration that killed the babies.

Many of the children I had seen in the campo had numerous scars on their legs and arms. Some of this was due to insects and some from lack of nutrition.

It would always bother me to see them allow the flies to walk around on the babies' faces and lips and usually only brushed them away if they got near the eyes.

Even the very basics of proper sanitation were not practiced. Most women in the campo didn't think of washing their hands much less keeping foods covered so that flies and other insects didn't take their portion prior to the baby getting any.

I decided to go back and start a prenatal and postnatal childcare clinic. I gathered up as many of the magazines as I could and took them with me. Without a clue how I was going to do it, I was happy to be headed back with a new mission in mind.

Lacking The Social Graces

After returning to my pueblo, I was so energized that I thought it was time I had a social life. The girl that I was first attracted to happened to be the one that cleaned the office. This was where our agency kept the supplies, made out the reports, and just hung around when we couldn't get out because of the rains.

She was a drop-dead knockout that had a three-year-old baby girl. Almost every day I would pick up a quart of milk or orange juice and then purposely drink only a cup or so and give the rest to her to take home to her little girl. I asked around, about her, and every one said to go for it. I was all set to ask her out and discovered that she was not divorced so I backed off.

Looking around, I decided one day while eating lunch, to ask the girl at the local restaurant. She was nice and I thought available. I asked her to the movies and she accepted.

Now, the movie theater in town was no bigger than about forty pews. It was really a store converted to a movie house. It did not have the sloping floor, individual seats or a nice large screen like most Americans are accustomed to. It had long narrow benches with no backs on them, and a screen about half the normal size. It looked like a bed sheet with tears in it, but for a few pesos, it was as much as one might expect.

If you weren't careful the guy next to you would elbow you to get more room. You also had to look out for the splinters on the pews.

The "Guns of Navarone" was playing. Of course, the only thing they could get were old movies no one in the U.S. wanted any more. Most were in black and white to boot and were subtitled which I didn't have to bother with unless I wanted to learn a few new Spanish words. I didn't care; it was a wonderful night and my first social engagement since Texas.

As we entered the theater all faces turned to us. I am sure they were wondering who the lucky (or unlucky) lady was with the gringo. The use of the name gringo was not used in a derogatory way, it was just a whole lot easier for most of them to call me that in lieu of "Kirk", which almost everyone had a difficult time pronouncing.

I was told by the training staff that the word gringo came from early in the history of Nicaragua when our soldiers occupied their country and in the best English they could muster would say "green go" which came out gringo in their pronunciation. The green referred to the color of the soldiers' uniforms and they wanted them out of their country.

Anyway, there was constant whispering, about, I assumed, the two of us, during the whole movie. I didn't care; it was entertaining to be watching a movie again no matter how old or what the circumstances.

After the movie we walked around awhile and talked. As the time passed, I was trying to figure out how I was going to say good night and if a kiss was going to work it's self in. I was completely taken by surprise as she kind of led the walk around to the room where I was now living.

I now had a room adjacent to the engineering office as I had had to leave the family. I couldn't really tell them why and they really weren't happy but it was either that, or face more health issues.

She asked to come in, and being as naive as I can sometimes be I invited her to do so, and then she started to undress. I stopped her, said I needed to take her home, and quickly ushered us out the door. I walked her to her house, said good night and off I trotted back to my place.

* * * *

I was sitting in my room when I heard a commotion across the street and looked out to see what was going on. To my anger I saw her and one of the Nicaraguan engineers that I work with beating her.

I ran across the street and grabbed him by the neck. With my fist raised to give him a pop, I realized there was absolutely no resistance on his part. I was so surprised by this that I didn't hit him. I think he saw the amount of anger in my face and knew I was capable of anything at that moment. His next response was to tell me that they hit the women in his country and I shouldn't interfere.

I remember saying no one in any country hits a woman and if I catch him at it again I'll show him what hitting is all about. The bigger problem was the next day; he was scared to come to work, and had talked to the head guy at the office about what had happened.

I could not believe the people in my office sided with this guy about being allowed to hit their women. It was not that they were man and wife; they had only been dating before I asked her out, something I had not been aware of and certainly would not have asked her out had I known.

The lead engineer, thinking he was doing his duty and macho thing, decided to give me a lecture on not interfering in their culture. He proceeded to tell me that the men in his country have the right to beat their women. This really got my dander up because in the discussion I would find out that men could beat their girl friends, mistresses and wives.

I was to find out that the guy who caused all this ruckus was already married to another woman in his home pueblo and that really popped my cork!

I noticed the office assistant and cleaning lady were very subdued and quiet as the discussion went on and I told them, then and there, that I would not tolerate it. The incident was reported to Peace Corps' main office, for which, while sympathetic to what went on; I was reminded to remain "apolitical". I wasn't sure at the time what apolitical really meant, but I would come to find out that it's impossible to remain so.

This incident, coupled with the health issues, would cause my requirement to leave the agency and as destiny would have it, move on to my next inspiration. I also had second thoughts about starting a social life.

It was a good thing that I had not asked the girl who cleaned the office out because her husband would have done who knows what to her. I decided the best way to help her out was to pay her to clean my room and do my laundry.

In Nicaragua your clothes are taken down to the local stream and beat on the rocks. I found that the only clothes I had that could make it past five months were those made in the U.S.A. Every thing else would be rags in no time flat. I was getting that great pre-washed denim look for just a few pesos and a couple of washings.

During the rainy season I found it necessary to pay to have my laundry ironed several times just to dry them out. The humidity would be so high that you constantly had that feeling you get just after running from the store parking lot to the car in a downpour with no umbrella. You feel this wet, sticky clinging of clothes and just want to rip them off and towel dry your body.

The irons were like those used here in the U.S. back in the days before electricity and weighed as much as a set of barbells and were heated on the stove first.

So ironing your clothes was no easy chore but well worth the cost.

Peace Corps Partnership Program

Peace Corps agreed that continuing with the agency would be counter productive. The engineers from the Nicaraguan agency wanted me gone and it would now be difficult for me to be myself instead of their perception of some "macho man". The last thing they wanted was a change in their macho status with the local women. Most of them had mistresses in the pueblo. I was what they considered a threat to the Nicaraguan male image. As if this problem wasn't enough, my legs were so infected by insect bites the Peace Corps didn't want me further exposed to malaria and typhoid, so they asked me to stay in the region but to come up with my own assignment.

No problem! I had already been talking with one of the local priests associated with the schools in the area so I had the resources for finding a new project. I eventually hooked up with a Catholic Priest (Father Andres) who asked if I could help out with desks, blackboards and supplies for a local school that he ran. I had gotten information on the "Peace Corps Partnership Program" and got to work writing a proposal to get funding. The way the program worked was, the Peace Corps Volunteer comes up with a proposal for a project, explains why the project is so badly needed, and how he will go about completing the project. The proposal, along with many others, is then sent to organizations, usually in the U.S. If they like what they see, they agree to fund the project.

The volunteer must write progress reports and give status updates of the project as it proceeds. The volunteer is also responsible to be the project manager, distributor of the monies and supplier of all receipts and documents throughout the project.

Perhaps the best thing about these programs was that 100 percent of the monies went to the project. There was no paying off Government officials or organizations for administrative costs. I was able to get my project accepted by an organization in Illinois called "Oak Park Council on International Affairs". Soon money was transferred to the Peace Corps for my use.

Father Andres, being a very well liked priest, was able to secure the wood necessary for the desks from someone the Nicaraguan Government would later claim was from the "Sandinista".

The Sandinistas were a revolutionary group trying to end a nearly 100-year reign of a very corrupt family rule called the Somosa's. The Somosa dictatorship was intense, brutal and without concern or adherence to the issues of human rights. Much later, the Regan administration termed the Sandinistas as "Freedom Fighters". The "Sandinista" gave us all the wood at cost, and labor was free from the pueblo people. Shortly before the desks were finished, this man, whom I had met and liked and who thought the world of Father Andres, was arrested and tortured to death by the Government.

I asked Father Andres how he knew that the man had been tortured and the Father told me that he had administered to the family and saw the mutilated body. I could tell from the Father's voice that I shouldn't pry because the horrific things done to the man had the father in tears.

My days of being "apolitical" would start to twist and turn inside my stomach, as more atrocities were committed in the months to follow. The desks were delivered and during the process I had taken photos of the village and children to go in my progress reports.

Father Andres had one of the local boys carve a copy of the Nicaraguan crest out of wood and I bought, with my money, some of the local artesian objects that were typical of the country and made a thank you package for our sponsor.

They were so delighted with what I sent, they wrote me and said it was the first time they had felt so rewarded for their efforts and planned to display the items in their office as a tribute to those who helped gather the money. I was very proud of that project and what it accomplished. It inspired me to move forward with the clinic project. I actually saw that it was possible for me, one man, to really make a difference.

* * * *

In Nicaragua most if not all, of the classrooms have only desks, chairs, blackboard and a teacher. They were totally lacking in what I call visual effects, not through any fault of their own, but a lack of resources and maybe just a little creativity.

I gathered as many of the National Geographic magazines as I could get my hands on from Peace Corps headquarters and the embassy, along with any other magazines that looked interesting.

I started to work on bringing some life to a lifeless classroom. I found at least two, and often times more, full-page pictures of people from other countries in almost every National Geographic. I cut these out and mounted them as a border going around the entire classroom. There were children, men, and women from all sorts of different countries and cultures. They really dressed up the room.

Next, I took out all the pictures of sea and land animals and mounted them on a four by eight sheet of plywood that I bought and made a map of the world. It was a colorful collage of sea animals for the ocean and land animals for the land areas. I mounted this on the opposite wall from the blackboard.

I even surprised the teachers with a few boxes of colored chalk that I had sent to me to help make it seem less drab when using the blackboard.   The teachers were amazed with the chalk, which was something they didn't seem to know existed. The looks on the kids' faces as they came in and saw their classroom that day told me this kind of project was worth pursuing in my spare time.

* * * *

I shifted my means of entertainment from any hopes of a social life to making kites for the kids in the pueblo. Before long, any one who wanted one got one, and of course, they kept showing up on my doorstep as word got around. Like most things, I like to do things in a big way and made one for myself. Like most men, I will remain a kid at heart as long as I live. My kite was over eighteen feet long and five feet wide. It had eight long streaming legs, two huge eyes and a smiling mouth. It looked like a giant purple octopus with its tentacles as the tail of the kite.

The kids and many of the adults in the pueblo thought it was a sight to behold. Once I got it in the air, and from then on, the kids thought I was great and the adults thought I was "el gringo loco".

* * * *

My next living quarters, after the exit from the engineering activity and not wanting to live right next door to them, was within a small house I shared with David, the other volunteer in the pueblo. He took pity on me and let me share rent and space. I dragged my scissor bed and clothes over to David's house, which had some "roommates" of its own that really gave me the creeps. I found it hard to sleep the first couple of weeks there. We shared the house with more scorpions and tarantulas than anyone could imagine.

David would catch them in jars and let them go outside. I would see them on the walls at night and worry that the spiders would drop down in the night or the scorpions would crawl in my boots.

David, being an agriculturalist, didn't see anything wrong with having them around, sort of like the guy that keeps a pet snake and takes pleasure out of feeding it live mice. I did not like seeing those things moving around, especially at night, and it brought back memories of having read Kafka's book "Metamorphosis" where a man turns into a spider. Just like anything else, you get used to it and accept the conditions you're in and don't seem to give a damn where they are, where they have been and where they might be heading.

I remember one night after David had had more than a few beers. He caught one of each critter, and put them in a jar together to see which would be left by morning. David watched them for hours hoping one or the other would start the fighting and even failed at his attempts to shake the jar and get them started. If they could communicate they were probably saying this is one sick human. No wonder the Gladiators of Roman history were humans. They are the only ones sick enough to do this for entertainment.

The scorpion won and all that was left of the much bigger spider were a few legs. That was gross. David did get cured of them being around when he forgot one morning to carefully check his boots and found his foot together with a scorpion. He didn't get stung and was lucky. I guess the scorpion was so horrified by the smell of David's feet the he forgot to sting.

* * * *

I started working on my clinic idea. I wrote nearly three hundred letters to every medical facility and pharmacy whose addresses I had found in the magazines that I had brought back from Peace Corps headquarters. I told them of my idea and asked for donations of medical equipment and medicines, vitamins and vaccinations specific to my cause.

The writing program was going so well for medical supplies that I decided to write to all the major league baseball clubs to see if they would be willing to donate any of their used equipment.

I explained who I was and where I was and what the proposed use of the equipment was for. To my surprise, and deep gratitude, the Seattle Mariners sent me rain jackets, caps, balls and bats. Peace Corps headquarters was pleasantly surprised when the equipment showed up and I got a special telegram to come and get them. It was my understanding that the club had made arrangements via the embassy to get them to me unpilfered.

Not one to stop while his luck was running, I started writing to publishers for books in Spanish. Again I was totally surprised and elated when books starting arriving from the main publishers in South America. I really wasn't holding out much hope for the

Latin publishers, but they were the most forthcoming. All in all I ended up with over a hundred books for all ages for the school.

The one American publisher that decided to help me out sent the most beautiful laminated animal pictures you could imagine but with the understanding that I would translate them into Spanish. They would, in turn, produce a copy in Spanish for me with the m having the right to sell them afterwards. Capitalism at its best but I didn't mind and got one of the local teachers to help me out.

Eventually, enough nursing and medical books showed up in Spanish which meant that I had the means to have midwife and nurses training classes if we had a teacher.

I asked the Peace Corps volunteer nurse in the nearby city if she would teach classes on how to be a midwife and the procedures for birthing after my clinic idea got off the ground and she was more than accommodating. All I had to do was let her know when and she would provide not only the training but also the materials to conduct the classes.

I thought I would go a step farther with the nurses training idea. She said that if she could review the books I had, and if she felt she could grasp the technical elements and communicate the technical Spanish terms, then no problem. Hey, anything was better than the practices currently being carried out. According to the volunteer, they were seeing many women brought to the hospital that had infections and other complications because of the current pueblo practices.

Another book that the Peace Corps recommended, that I purchased in quantity for the pueblo, was called "Donde No Hay Doctor" which means, "Where there is no doctor". This book was incredible and designed for illiterate people with pictures of what to do or not do in medical circumstances. Why it even showed the right way to wipe with a corncob so you wouldn't tear up the hind-part.

Things were going so well and getting the mail was like Christmas every day. I never knew from one day to the next which of the letters I had written would be answered or what wonderful goodie for the clinic would show up.

And The Most Precious Of These Are The Children

The drought that summer was bad. I saw in my field trips, putting in wells and latrines, that the lack of food was severe. Some people were pulling leaves off the trees and making soup out of them because of a lack of food.

It is one thing to see a starving child on TV. It is another to see one in person. The haunting look of their sunken eyes as they look at you, the sensations you feel because they don't appear to be human because they are so stringy in body composition.

Years later I would see Sally Struthers on TV surrounded by starving children with such sincerity in her pleading voice and teary eyes as she asked for help for the children. I knew, watching that commercial that she had been there. I believe the program she was trying to assist was "Save the Children" Foundation that was not unlike the "Foster Parents Plan" which I had participated in.

There's a place in the heart where one can't help being torn to shreds wanting to do so much yet feeling helpless, and in trying to get others to see and feel what you do at that moment. It is one thing to hear, to read and to see on TV but it is so different when it is literally right in front of you.

* * * *

A Baptist group from Alabama showed up in our village one day and heard about me and asked if I would show them around and interpret.

I thought it would be a great privilege to do that because here was a religious group that could only mean well in their intentions. So, I didn't think much of it when they showed up in their air-conditioned four-wheel vehicles.

I remember a few of them looking as though they did not want these people to come too close to them. It was probably from fear that they might contract disease or something from them. Still I held out hopes that by the time I finished with them even the coldest and hardest of hearts would melt into my plan.

I took them to some of the sections of the pueblo that I thought would move their hearts. At the end of the day I helped them get their souvenir machetes. As the time for them to get back in their vehicles and return to the city approached, I made my move. I told them about the desperate need for food and medicine as they surely had seen during the day. I let them know that being a Peace Corps Volunteer, should they want to go back to their church and raise money for this purpose, I would make sure that every last penny got spent on food and medicine and nothing else.

I was sure this was a great plan but I was not prepared for the response I got back. As long as I live, I will never forget their words **"these people don't need food in their stomachs or clothes on their backs, all they need is Jesus in their hearts"**.

I was so stunned I could not talk, and did not reply. I thought to myself, "Tell that to one of those starving children you saw today as you ride back to the nice hotel in your air-conditioned vehicle and eat your meal in the dining room tonight".

I knew that somewhere in the bible Jesus says to bring the children unto him for they are the most precious. I also knew at that moment I must be right about being judged one day on what you could have done and didn't. This would tear my faith, as would other incidents that followed.

* * * *

As the end of the year neared, so did the end of David's tour. He planned to return to the United States by land through Honduras, El Salvador, Guatemala, and Mexico and asked if I would like to accompany him part way as a vacation.

I did, and had a great time going to see the Mayan ruins of Copan in Honduras and Tikal out in the Guatemalan jungle.

One afternoon, as we were eating at a restaurant in Guatemala City, a precious little girl of about ten walked up to our table and asked if we wanted to buy some little dolls she had made. They were about three inches high, looked like large wooden clothespins with typical native clothes and painted faces. Well, looking at her I could not resist and we bargained back and forth and I gave her what I knew was a good deal. David just laughed but knew I was a sucker for things like that. The little girl left quite content and David and I continued eating our meal.

It was only about ten minutes later when she returned with a hand full of more dolls and her little sister of about five with her hands full. We struck a new deal and David helped out by buying some and told me we better get up and get out before she returned again. I had dozens of these dolls and figured I would give them out to the kids back in my pueblo as Christmas presents.

When it came time for David to head up into Mexico and me to head back to Nicaragua it was sad and lots of things ran through my mind. I wondered if I could make it a full two years like he did. Where would I live now and what was I doing with my life? By the time I got back I knew I had to concentrate on the clinic and put the loneliness aside.

I returned in time for Christmas and gave my dolls to the girls in the street and for the first time had longings for home. Christmas there had no trees, no lights, no exchanging of gifts and just seemed like another day. There was a boy in the pueblo that would shine shoes to help his family. He was about nine or ten years old. I would always get my boots shined no matter if they needed it or not because it was only about two pennies and I knew it helped out.

I asked him what he got for Christmas and with a happy smile said "apples and oranges". If I remember right I got my boots shined many times that day because they kept getting dusty.

* * * *

I was starting to feel that Peace Corps service was as much about learning about ourselves as it was contributing to helping other people. Our actions or expressions were known throughout the pueblo with every breath we took and every action we attempted.

You can make a difference by example and by just trying and caring to try. Your emotions go for a ride, you feel will never end, with as many twists and turns as any roller coaster could give.

I was starting to feel the stress of my assignment in just a short time. Not a stress of work so much as of trying to deal with such a variety of experiences. I could not ever have thought to have faced in my lifetime such a wide range of experiences, emotions, disappointments, and successes.

Ride em Up Movies

My social life was not quite at an end because I met a girl, who together with a friend of hers, was helping to take care of a little orphaned girl. I knew at once this had to be an exceptional person to do such a thing.

We started dating and life was a lot easier because Carmen was from a northern pueblo, had no family, friends or ties apart from her one girlfriend there in Condega. So I didn't have to worry about beatings and gossip, well... maybe gossip.

Carmen and I were together eating one afternoon and I was running the clinic idea by her. I was looking for ideas on how to go about getting the town folk involved in helping. We were sitting there when the little orphaned girl came crying because the other kids in school had been making fun of her. It seemed she did not have the uniform required by the school.

Carmen and I struck a deal that I would buy the material; she would sew the uniform and agree to help me on the clinic project.

I knew Carmen would have helped me with the clinic anyway but I also knew she would have felt uncomfortable about buying the uniform, so it was the best way I could come up with to not put her on the spot.

Concentrating on the clinic effort and Carmen became my driving force. The first thing I did was to open a bank account in the name of "Clinica de Condega" which I did with only about twenty dollars in pesos of my own money.

What I hoped for worked, and within only hours, word was all around town. Next, Carmen and I brainstormed about how to raise money from an impoverished area. We decided that just selling typical street foods and soda on the street would not amount to much and neither of us had the time to do that anyway.

The idea of putting on a dance at the "casa comunal", which is a public meeting place used by the pueblo, would be difficult at best. I was worried about the campesino's coming into town and drinking and then getting into fights at the dance.

Friday nights were usually a big night out for the campesinos. They would ride into town, down a considerable amount of liquor and whip out the machetes. At least they couldn't afford guns or we would have had a"shoot 'em up" on Friday nights. I figured I better set my plans for a Saturday or Sunday, whatever the event, in order to not interfere with the macho male night out. Besides, they probably wouldn't bring the wife and kids if it were a Friday.

I definitely needed a form of entertainment, which would be free, attract the entire family and then, at the function I could sell coke and food.

I figured if I went down to Peace Corps headquarters then maybe someone there could give me some pointers on what other volunteers may have come up with in the past or things they may have tried. So I got on a bus the next day and headed to the capital. Unfortunately it was a dry well from the standpoint of help. I asked Peace Corps if the embassy had any resources I could use and they told me to go over and see. Upon arriving at the embassy they allowed me access to their library, which had, of all things, educational movies in Spanish. I was thrilled and allowed to check out the 16mm movie "Universe" in color and in Spanish, I headed back to the pueblo.

Father Andres had a projector so I was in business. I built a screen out of a bed sheet with a wood support frame and set it on the hillside. The biggest problem I had was to find an extension cord long enough to run the projector.

Carmen and I did a test run with what we had and it was fantastic. We set about making posters advertising that we would be showing a free movie for everyone, outside, with the proceeds from the sale of food and drinks going to the clinic.

Carmen took care of getting the raw materials and recipes to the women who had volunteered to help us. She then told them how to prepare and get the food ready for sale. She was a phenomenal organizer. I will never forget her.

The night of the movie we had people all over the place and campesino's from all over rode in to see a free movie. It could have passed for a rodeo show there were so many horses. The people were accustomed to watching old U.S. films, dubbed with subtitles, and mostly in black and white. To see one in color, in Spanish and free was not something to be missed. Sales of food were going great which we sold at the local going rate.

The night could not have been more perfect. It was a moonless night, warm and all the stars you could want to see. We had purposely set up on a hillside so there would be no bad seat in the house provided you liked sitting in the grass. It almost looked like an amphitheater but without a few of the ruffles and amenities.

I was about to introduce these people to even more amazing things that were above them that night. I had not previewed the entire movie and could not have been more amazed myself after seeing it. It showed the different galaxies in colors, the birth of a star and so on, all in Spanish.

After the movie was over the people applauded and asked if I could show it again. One very elderly lady came up to me, crying, and told me it was the most beautiful thing she had seen and thanked me a million times. For Carmen and I, it was a success beyond our wildest dreams and we raked in the money. I would repeat this process a number of times in the coming months and the second showing was of Jacques Cousteau filming under the ocean.

We now had the credibility that the clinic was real, so I proceeded to the next step, which was to organize the pueblo and elect a board of directors. Carmen and I set about letting the people know that I wanted a town meeting.

I went to the town Priest and asked to use the "Casa Comunal" which was next to the church and belonged to the pueblo for just such town meetings. To my surprise the Priest told me NO! When I asked why, he would not give me an answer so I figured I must not have kissed someone's ring.

I asked one of the more prominent people in the pueblo to intercede on my behalf and help convince the Priest to allow us to use the casa. I found out, later, that he did so only after having a meeting of his own. It seems the town folk were told that I was not to be taken seriously and that building a clinic in the pueblo was a monumental task, which would surely fail.

The night of the town meeting, the majority of the people showed up and I spent the better part of the first hour dispelling the Priest's idea that the clinic was not possible. I was outraged to think a man of God had so little faith for a mission so important.

I explained to the people that if man could put another man on the moon than we certainly could put together the resources necessary to build a clinic.

All I was asking for was a place to bring pregnant women prior to birth for vitamins and classes on child care, birth the baby at the clinic in sterile conditions, and follow up post-partum care with necessary shots and care for the babies. What seemed so hard to many seemed so easy to me.

That night we would elect a board of directors and a fine group they would become.

A Hospital For A Clinic

The board of directors felt that every one in the pueblos surrounding us, which amounted to two others, would also benefit from the clinic and that we should go door to door taking up collections. I didn't feel good about this and preferred to do things along the line of the movies.

I felt it was more important that they gave because they wanted to, not because they were asked. I certainly did not want the poor to feel compelled to give when there was little or nothing to give.

Most of these people were struggling to get by and I knew, given that the clinic was something for their children, they would want to give regardless of their circumstances. Almost anywhere you go a parent will do whatever they can for their children without regard for their own personal needs. It is a fact of human nature and is a dominant trait in women. One of the board members agreed with me because the poor were already giving what little they had for the collection that the Priest was taking up in the nearby pueblo for a bell tower for the church.

One of my problems was that I could be rather naive when it comes to what I perceive to be the right thing to do, so I went to see the Priest about the clinic project. The Priest agreed to meet with me. I believe he had heard about some of the things I had done for Father Andres and figured his time for getting something was at hand. Instead, I explained that if he could see it in his heart to use the bell tower money he had already collected for the clinic, that we could reach many of the mothers and children that were currently in need.

Again, I would be floored with the response from what I felt was supposed to be a holy man. He not only said no, but also insisted that the church also needed a new coat of paint and that I was not to interfere with the people's giving to the "Lord". I explained that Jesus taught from a hillside and that the purpose of the church was to unite people in his name and could be from a tent as well as a building. The Priest threw me out. He was going to have his bell tower.

At this point in my life, I was starting to wonder if it was just I. Was I so blind? Should people suffer in the name of the Lord? Was resurfacing the parking lot of a church in the U.S. more important than feeding the hungry and caring for the sick? Although both my grandmother and grandfather were ministers and I was trained not to question such things, I was now being shaken to the roots of my religious faith.

* * * *

A member of the board of directors was a prominent lady in the pueblo who ran a local goods store on the main street and had a number of window display boxes.

She agreed to allow Carmen and I to fill one of the boxes with a clinic theme to help bring awareness and promote the concept.   Carmen and I got to work right away and put some of the books along with medicines and other objects that would attract attention.   The idea was "a clinic coming soon to a pueblo near you".

This turned out to be very effective and rarely a day went by when we didn't alter the window display to keep drawing peoples' attention to what we were trying to do.

* * * *

Another effort that I started was to petition the United States Agency for International Development (USAID) for assistance.   This was to become a very labor and paper intensive effort.

We made arrangements to meet with one of the in-country personnel to explain the project and where we stood with it up to that point. By the time I answered all their questions, I realized they were a bureaucracy within a bureaucracy. They were insisting that I work with, and involve, the local government, which I didn't think was going to work. USAID seemed interested and wanted to participate but had their hands tied by the way they were allowed to operate in country.

In the end, I had to abandon any participation by them because of politics. Especially given the current state of the country politics, I wanted to stay independent, and the board agreed.

* * * *

However, things started to pick up at a faster rate because the hundreds of letters I had written were being answered with favorable responses.

One in particular made my jaw drop. I was not quite prepared when the "Pan American Foundation" sent me a notice asking if I would consider the total equipment necessary for a small hospital, which would include two operating rooms.

The package the foundation wanted to send was designed as a field hospital unit just like those used in the Korean War. In essence, it was a Mobile Army Surgical Hospital or MASH unit. I had started this whole idea with just the thought of a small three or four bed clinic to birth children, and now, it seemed to be growing before my eyes. This worried me for many reasons, mostly because staffing and operating something of this magnitude was beyond this pueblo's means and capability.

I did not want to prove the Priest right, not because we could not build it, but because we couldn't maintain it. I immediately met with the board and found them to be in favor of moving forward with the grandiose idea while I was determined to keep it simple.

In very little time, the word leaked out, and I do mean way out. I had a late night visit from one of the Sandinista leaders. We struck a deal that he would leave the clinic and me out of his war, and I would agree that medical attention would be available to anyone regardless of political preference, should the war warrant it.

I also received a telegram that my presence was requested at the Ministry of Health in the capital. At my earliest convenience, I was to let them know when I could make myself available for discussions regarding my "hospital" project. I was never so overwhelmed and bummed.

I went to the capital that week and met with some of the Government's top officials. I explained that I was not building a hospital but just a clinic and why. They encouraged me to build a hospital and then they would take control.

I explained that I had a local board of directors and wanted it to be a tri-pueblo project and would more than welcome the ministry's involvement in supplying medicines, vaccinations, vitamins and such.

I left with the typical bureaucratic uncertainty that government officials are renowned for. At least with the Sandinistas it was straightforward but now I didn't know if the ministry was going to insist they be involved or throw me out of the country for not allowing them to participate. The leaking of that information did have its good points. A nearby landowner donated ten acres of land, which was visible from, and had easy access to, the Pan American Highway. It was also easy to get to from all three pueblos.

The down side was that he donated a very tall hill for which he wanted to see the "clinic" at the top. His idea was for all to see the splendor of the clinic.

I insisted that it was difficult for nine-month pregnant women to walk up a hill like that but he just laughed and said that Nicaraguan women were like mules, they could handle anything no matter the conditions. I could not argue with getting free land so figured I would work some kind of shuttle service from the bottom up.

Another important individual to hear the news was a brick manufacturer in the next city, who wanted the publicity of being the supplier, so agreed to provide all of the cement and bricks at cost. This saved us a lot of money.

* * * *

Another experience I had during this time was to live through the nightmare of a 7.7 magnitude earthquake! It happened at about 1:30 in the morning and shook the place like a pan of popcorn on a burner.

There were two factors, other than timing, that made things worse. One was that there was no moon, so it was very dark and no one had time to dress so everyone was in various degrees of undress; most being in just their underwear. I must have been a sight in my underwear trying to put my boots on, as they were the only things I grabbed on my way out! Maybe I had watched too many westerns and had the idea that it was more important to die with my boots on than with anything else!

The one thing that scared the bajeebers out of me was the people screaming. Many of these people had already experienced earthquakes and were scared to death. It seemed like the women mustered up their most blood curdling sounds and just let them rip.

Because I had studied geology in college, I was aware that the aftershock was only seconds away and would probably be more destructive. When it did happen, the whole ground felt like it was rolling under my feet!

12

A Social Revolution

I had not paid too much attention to the Sandinista efforts because I was trying to be apolitical. Besides, the clinic had my undivided attention. Things started to intensify in the pueblo to the point I was no longer able to ignore what was going on or about to happen. It got to the point that every night the town's people would burn things in the main road at night and chant things like "Por una Nicaragua liberada, una guierra prolongada" which rhymed in Spanish but meant "for a free Nicaragua, a prolonged war".

It was no longer safe to walk the streets at night because the military would show up in jeeps and start shooting, either above the heads of the people or at them. Everyone would run in one direction or another to escape. Several nights I found myself running down the road, not because I was participating, but because I needed to get from one place to another for food, meetings or whatever. It is amazing how fast one can run when the sounds of bullets are whizzing about and people are screaming. These weren't just men being shot at, but also women and children of all ages.

This started to interfere with the clinic project and the guard station banned my movie nights so I cut a deal with the local movie house and started having them there. Participation was dropping off badly because people were being instructed by the Sandinistas to store food and supplies for the coming offensive. Movies were no longer a part of their budget. The campesinos were no longer willing to risk riding into town with the jeeps showing up at unexpected times. The guards had become intolerant of their drinking and drunken behavior. They figured that because they lived in the mountains they had privilege to the whereabouts or movements of the Sandinistas. Therefore, as a campesino you would risk being hauled away for questioning.

As the revolution progressed, everything ground to a halt. No one was able to concentrate on anything but the offensives that were taking place in different areas of the country.

Carmen got word from her relatives that the military was bombing their city, nearby us, and the jeeps showing up at all hours of the night were now targeting the people.

Peace Corps was in a panic because the volunteers were reporting in from all over that the situation was getting scary and they felt we were all at risk.

Just as I was thinking things couldn't get much worse for me, a bunch of mercenaries showed up and asked me to help escort them around the nearby areas. I was amazed to think they thought I might just be willing to traipse though the jungle with them like some Indian scout. I looked at them totally dumbfounded and said, "look, get away from me. Don't come near me again or your going to get me killed".

We had heard that the government had put out contracts for mercenaries-for-hire to help supplement the National Guard. Up to this point, the only thing in our pueblo was a small guard station manned by only two guards, who would no longer venture out of the station unless the jeeps showed up from the nearest next city.

The last thing I needed was the Sandinistas thinking I was helping the other side. I also cared dearly for the people in the pueblo and wanted these mercenaries gone. They just stayed that day and then disappeared into the mountains.

The most depressing thing to see was the teenagers using stones and slingshots against the automatic weapons of the military. I just couldn't understand it. They even started bending nails into a configuration that when thrown on the Pan American Highway would always land in an upright position to flatten the tires of the jeeps.

This was cleaver but also resulted in local transportation coming to a stand still because the buses kept getting flat tires. At this point, we couldn't go anywhere even if we wanted to, or the bus would drive slowly with a spotter in front to look for the shiny objects.

After weeks of this increasing intensity, a determining point in my staying in Nicaragua arrived. The Sandinistas asked me if I had a problem with them blowing up the Pan American Highway just outside of town where the main bridge was. The Sandinistas were true to their word and did not want to interfere with my efforts so they just told me what their plan was.

Talk about some soul searching being done! I knew it would mean that I would be in the middle of some intense fighting and cut off from any possible rescue from the South.

The National Guard needed the Pam American highway to be able to transport troops to the north and without it one would have to take dirt roads that were nearly inaccessible during the rains.

Believe it or not, when you're in certain situations, you will react much differently than you might think at hearing about it and doing what makes sense. I was ready to die there and told the Sandinistas to do what they had to do.

I called Peace Corps headquarters and informed them that if they didn't get the northern volunteers out soon they would need helicopters, and I knew that wasn't going to happen. The United States government had installed the cruel military regime and sent Somosa and his son through West Point. The C.I.A. had backed this government from the beginning.

One of the main complaints of the Nicaraguan people was the U.S. ships showing up in the ports with military hardware on board. Our guards in the pueblo went from having rifles to automatic weapons over night.

They were also getting sophisticated weapons, the likes of which I had never seen. One in particular drew my attention because it looked like an automatic shotgun. It actually had what looked like a conveyer belt that fed shotgun shells into the rifle. And if they weren't U.S. built, where in blue blazes were they coming from?

Then president Jimmy Carter didn't seem to know which way to turn and may have had very poor information from his advisors, which allowed the situation to fester. Instinctively I knew something was about to happen that would seriously affect me.

* * * *

My last night in Nicaragua was almost my last night on earth. What started out like a normal night with the burning and chanting in the streets became one of the longest nights of my life.

I was coming back from eating, and when I turned one of the corner streets, there was a mob of people running at me. I knew that could only mean one thing. As I ducked down another street I saw the military jeep go by and the shooting start.

I took off like an Olympic sprinter and found myself running into another mob. This time, not only were the bullets flying, but there were explosions. Once again I reversed direction and remember thinking, "which way do I run?" The military was trying to pin us in.   Every direction we tried to run would be cut off.   People were screaming and pounding on doors for the owners to let them in for shelter.

I was in a mess and knew it. If I gave up I was sure the military wouldn't care who I was and probably do those things you only read about in magazines.

By now, President Carter had decided not to back the government any more and most of the military probably felt if you're not with them, you must be against them.

I was well aware that I knew too much about the Sandinistas for it to be in my best interest should the military interrogate me. So I kept running and ran right into a smoking, handmade bomb lobbed in front of me. I literally flew up against the wall of the house where I was and was not sprayed by any of its flying shrapnel. As I turned to run the other way a military jeep drove up behind me.

I managed to get to a nun's house and pleaded for shelter. She assisted me, hid me and let me stay the night. I knew instinctively I could not go back to my place. Morning would take forever to come and the screaming and shooting would not subside until the early morning hours. When morning did arrive the military had left and it was safe to go back to my place.

I was not sure what I was going to do. To this day I don't know why I did it, but I spent that morning putting tags on my belongings as to whom I wanted things to go to in the event of my death.

Every thing was answered for me later that morning when the Peace Corps deputy country director showed up in his vehicle with three other volunteers aboard. I was told I had ten minutes to grab only what I needed because we were headed to Honduras. I knew by the terrified look on the other's faces that we were leaving for good.

Carmen had come to see me that morning and some how she knew that she would not see me again. She was there when the Peace Corps vehicle pulled up and the last thing I saw, as I looked back, was her standing there crying. Part of me wanted to leave and part did not. I felt afraid for those left behind and sad because I also knew that it was good-bye for good.

* * * *

Carmen and I would stay in communication during the next several months after I left Nicaragua. The economy had become unbearable for those left behind so I would send her money when I could.

I don't know what ever happened to her but all communication from her just stopped. Maybe her writing to the "Gingo" caused problems. In retrospect, her getting American money could not have looked too favorable.

The democratic Sandinistas, which Carmen and I knew, were mostly killed in the first stages of war so they would have been no protection for her. Had President Carter not taken so long to decide whom to support, things may have been different.

Maybe President Regan would not have to subject the country to further bloodshed and warring by searching out those democratic Sandinistas known to Americans as the freedom fighters, and to me as friends.

13

Crossing The Border

The ride out of the pueblo was a fast one. For each mile we traveled north we knew we were further into Sandinista territory and did not know what to expect. We still had one more volunteer to retrieve on the Northern border prior to crossing.

We reached the other volunteer and then headed for the border during the daylight hours so risk was at a minimum. We were treated like celebrities at the border crossing of Honduras because the embassy had called ahead to clear us for the crossing.

I don't remember any of our belongings being searched but then again we really didn't have much to search through. All my belongings, including two new pairs of boots that I recently had made for me, were left behind with notes on them. That night we were taken to volunteers' houses and dropped off, much like what happened when we first arrived in Nicaragua. The next morning we were taken to the Peace Corps headquarters in Honduras and told that we might be flown back to the capital of Nicaragua in a few days. We were totally amazed by that statement. From what we had heard and seen prior to the evacuation we could not believe things were going to be over that quickly. It seemed that Peace Corps headquarters in Washington was getting its' Intel from both the embassy and State Department. Both were either oblivious to what was occurring, or thought they had pumped enough support into the existing Government to squash the uprising. The Peace Corps volunteers were also aware that there was a difference of opinion between the country ambassador and Peace Corps director on just how bad things were getting. At least the volunteers were aware of the situation because of living in it, whereas the embassy personnel were not. I had seen kids throwing rocks at guards, who were shooting at them with automatic weapons and knew that it would be a prolonged war.

Week after week went by and every day there was little or no information about what was going to happen to us. Finally the day came and the announcement was made that the volunteers were to pack their bags. We would be flown back to the capital of Nicaragua. After getting ready to go we would again be put on hold.

All volunteers in country were now in the capital region and space was becoming a problem. But then, the attacks and explosions of buses, cars and buildings was becoming a serious problem.

During week three of the evacuation, I accidentally ran into the president of the board of directors for the clinic. We had coffee together and he explained how he had escaped to Honduras and that the doctor and two other members of the board had been tortured and executed. My heart sank and I knew my clinic did not stand a chance without my return.

By the same token I knew that my original dream of building a pre and postnatal childcare clinic was fading in a war torn country. The people would need a makeshift hospital instead of a clinic and they would be too worried about staying alive to give any attention to construction of a clinic. I did not see a positive solution in the foreseeable future.

* * * *

I was frustrated about not knowing what was going to happen and tired of doing nothing every day. One night I decided to go to the local park to sit and think. Not long after sitting there, I noticed a nine or ten year old girl with her four or five year old little brother going through the trashcans in the park. To my horror, they were eating what they would find.

I walked over and asked her where her mother was and she replied that she had been run over by a car two years before. "Your father," I replied, "where is he?" She did not know her father. There was only her and her brother, no other relatives. I told her and her brother to follow me over to the local McDonalds.

As I walked in, she stood outside. I motioned her in and said, "Listen, I will buy you as much as you and your brother can eat and than we will get some to go as well". As we stood in line one of the workers ran up and started pushing her and the brother out the door. I stopped him and said they were with me and we intended to eat. He was upset and did not know how to respond to this gringo, and the other customers were looking at the children with disgust.

What the others saw were two street urchins, dirty and tattered. What I saw were two hungry children. I got our food and we sat down and ate. I told them to ignore the others who were looking at us and that they were looking at me because I was different. This made sense to them, so then they wolfed down them cheese burgers! When they couldn't eat any more, I bought another couple bags of burgers and fries and we headed out the door.

I told her I would walk her and her brother back home. It was then that it hit me like a ton of bricks that I had no idea where that was.

We walked, with her leading the way, and when we arrived, I was not prepared for what I saw. Her house was a cardboard box along with many others in an alley of a distant street. The roof and sides had various scraps of foil from cigarette wrappers and tin lids from cans stuck to them to help resist the rains and keep the cardboard from getting wet. Inside were a few tattered clothes and a rag bed. She and her brother crouched down and went in with their bags of food in hand. I peered in and saw their thankful eyes looking back at me. Knowing that I would have to turn and walk away, back to what I had, and knew it was something I would never forget.

I walked for hours, crying, not knowing what to do or how to help. I wondered how much more I would have to see and feel before this was over. The next morning I asked what facilities were available for abandoned children. I was told that there were insufficient facilities in the capital area to deal with so many. I was also told by a Honduran Peace Corps volunteer that in many ways the ones in the street preferred the street to the conditions of the centers.

I wondered how it was that the United States, which had given an untold amount of monies to the Middle East, could leave its neighbors so uncared for. I would learn that it is mostly a matter of political and economic excuses.

* * * *

We were in the main office when the news finally came about our assignments. All of the volunteers, except for me, were given a choice of either being flown back to the capitol or reassignment. I was told that because so little time was left of my assignment that I could be flown back to the U.S. and given a completion of tour. I elected, instead, to be reassigned.

I did not find out until after I was reassigned that Peace Corps had not intended to send me back to Nicaragua. The reason was because the night before I had escaped to Honduras, the night I hid at the nun's, the National Guard was conducting a house-to-house search for me. They considered me a target.One of the female volunteers came to me and asked if she should return. She was scared, for safety reasons, of going back but like most dedicated volunteers wanted to do her part and complete her assignment. I remember telling her that while I could not say whether she should go back or not, if it were my choice, I would return.

She did return and I was informed later that she had been captured and raped by the National Guard. I felt somehow responsible for her and never forgave myself for the advice I gave to her. I wondered if I had only been more negative and less gung-ho for going back, maybe she would have made a different decision.

* * * *

I was asked by the Honduras Peace Corps staff if I would take an assignment in Honduras or El Salvador and elected instead to wait and see if they would have one in South America.

I was still holding on in the back of my mind to get to Chile, which was my original desire. I was asked on the third day if I would go to Columbia. I said no.

At last, without saying a word, and having resolved to just go home, I was asked if I would consider taking an assignment in Valparaiso, Chile. My response was immediate and decisive, YES!

* * * *

I was flown to the U.S. for an R&R prior to the reassignment. My parents thought I had completely lost my mind and encouraged me to look for employment in the Washington D.C. area. I somehow knew that my destiny lay elsewhere and I looked forward to my departure to Chile.

Chapter 14

Making The Transition

On the twentieth day of October 1978 I was flown to Santiago, Chile to do a two week orientation. Santiago is the capital and main city in Chile. It is a beautiful city and has the normal conveniences of a modern U.S. city.

I had just come from the jungle and knew that Peace Corps did not want to do jungle assignments back to back so I was pleased, but by the same token, felt that the goals of Peace Corps were being stretched in a place so modern. I soon found out that this was not the case and would understand why Peace Corps has a brother program called VISTA which operates here in the United States. Right after arriving in Chile, I learned that the American Embassy contacted the Nicaraguan Peace Corps office about a shipment of medical supplies that had shown up in the Port of

Corinto, Nicaragua. The Nicaraguan authorities wouldn't release the shipment without my authorization, since I had initially petitioned them for the clinic. I made arrangements, via the embassies of both countries (Nicaragua and Chile), to release the supplies to the order of nuns that had helped to hide me the night before my departure from Nicaragua. This was the same order that later had three of their nuns murdered, sending the U.S. into action and brought world opinion to bear on Central America.

* * * *

Another situation I ran into right from the first day in Chile was to discover that Spanish isn't spoken the same in each Spanish speaking country! It seemed that for each word I had learned in Nicaragua, there was a different one in Chile. Like "strawberry" in one country was "frutilla" and in the other it was "fresa"; avocado was "aguacate" in one and "palta" in the other. The Chilean Spanish was more traditional Castillian.

It was also a much smoother language in Chile and seemed like most words ended in "ito" which means "little" and is a kinder, more genteel way of expressing ones words.

* * * *

One week after arrival, all the other in-country volunteers and I were put on alert for possible evacuation. There I was, wondering if I had jumped from the frying pan into the fire. What was taking place was a massive troop build up along the border between Argentina and Chile. For centuries, there had been a dispute over ownership of some islands that lay to the south of both countries. Things were coming to a head just as I was arriving.

Argentina was preparing to go to war with Chile. They would have been successful had it not been for Chile's request for intervention from the Organization of American States.

There is a treaty between North and South American Nations that should one country ever is attacked, then the others will come to its aid. Based on this treaty, Costa Rica, a Central American country just South of Nicaragua, does not even bother to have a national army.

Because Argentinean troops had already crossed some of the Southern borders of Chile, the U.S. dispatched a fleet to the coast of Chile and told Argentina to cease its aggression. Had there been a war it would have been Goliath (Argentina), picking on David (Chile), without the benefit of a slingshot.

* * * *

Another item that I was briefed on, in the first two weeks, were the political problems between Chile and the U.S. It seemed that when the U.S. Central Intelligence Agency organized the military coup against the Chilean Government then in power, they did not expect the power to turn on them instead of rolling over to U.S. pressure. Consequently, Chile had one of the worst human rights violation dockets at the time by then President Agusto Pinoche.

I decided this time I would try my hardest to avoid any political discussions or anything that may have appeared to be political by anyone's standard, but again, would fail miserably.

* * * *

My country Peace Corps supervisor had made prior arrangements with a family he knew in Vina del Mar where I could rent a room and decided to go with me to the site. He decided that we should take the train instead of the bus.

From Santiago to Vina is only about 120 miles so I booked tickets for him and me on the train leaving at five in the afternoon. Because he knew the family and was going to stay overnight I figured it would be an easy intro to my new living quarters.

To my displeasure, my supervisor handed me the directions to the house and announced he would not be able to make it. I turned in his ticket and boarded the train for what I thought would be just a two-hour train ride.

I arrived at two o'clock the next morning, and there I was, in a strange city banging on the door of a family I had never met. After waking them, and a few disgruntled comments from the father of the family, I was shown my room and settled in for the night. The next morning I inquired as to the monthly rent and almost fell off my chair as the father announced it would be equivalent to my entire Peace Corps allotment. I was not sure if this was the father's way of showing his displeasure at me for showing up at that ungodly hour of the night or whether he thought I was some rich American.   Surely my supervisor had informed him of our status.   No matter which the circumstance, I decided right then and there that I was not going to have a repeat family arrangement like I had in Nicaragua.

* * * *

That morning I headed to my site, Valparaiso, which is adjacent to the beautiful port city of Vina del Mar.   I was to be a clinical psychologist with the Casa de Menores, which means the "house of the minors".

This was an evaluation and staging center for minor children who were runaways, those suffering from child abuse, orphaned, or any other of a myriad of circumstances (drugs, prostitution, criminal, etc.). My job was to be the full time psychologist for the center and work with the resident child psychologist who visited the center twice a week.

After introductions at the Casa de Menores, I explained my living arrangements to the director of the center and that I needed other accommodations quickly. I told him I would prefer to live with a poor family that could use my help. The director seemed to understand me right off the bat and arranged for me to rent a small room with a very poor family, which consisted of a single mom trying to raise her one son by herself. This was ideal. My room was about six feet by six with a bed and dresser, and again, a curtain door.

While the house had running water and electricity, I was to find out later that it was unavailable at certain times of the day and night and usually when I wanted it the most.

In Nicaragua, the showering with only cold water was not an issue because the climate was tropical. However, in Chile, with cold Antarctic waters, this was another story! Every time I took a shower, it looked like I was stepping on hot coals and dancing the rumba. After a few minutes and with every nerve in my body having snapsized a few million times, I would just take it like a man.

I didn't realize at first that I was to occupy the only bedroom in the house. The mother and her son had been in the process of fixing up the storage area behind the house for their bedroom so that I could have the other one.

I knew they needed the money but they would not allow me to switch rooms with them even when I insisted they needed the larger room. For fear of upsetting the balance of things, I didn't push the issue too far so we agreed on a fair price and I was "home" again. I was an instant hit with the small children in the pueblo and a constant source of entertainment for them. One of the friends of my new family was a young mother with a set of very young twins.

One day, being tired of the usual pueblo life, I decided to take the kids to the movies to see a Disney movie that was playing. I put the word out to get permission from their parents and invited all those that usually hung around. About fifteen kids showed up but no twins.

Rene, the teenage son of my landlady, helped me in a most impressive way. Not only did he help get all the kids on the bus but also he told the bus driver that we were on an excursion in the care of a Peace Corps volunteer who worked at the Casa de Menores.

This got us a reduced rate on the bus fare! I'm sure Rene was playing an angle but it did save us quite a bit of money for the bus and then also, for the tickets to get into the movies when he used the story again.

I bought everyone popcorn and sodas which, like here in the U.S., was more expensive than the whole rest of the trip. I figured these kids didn't have this opportunity often so we had to do it up right.

The next day, when the mother of the twins came over, I mentioned that we had missed them on our outing and wondered why they weren't with us. She responded that she didn't have clothing nice enough for them to wear on such an outing and didn't want them to feel embarrassed by the other children.

I, being a humble and unconcerned person for others appearances, found it strange to try to comprehend what some people had to consider when I had been brought up with all the necessities and conveniences of a "normal" life.

I knew her children were looking forward to the outing, and in doing what she thought best, created a conflict for her in trying to explain to her children why they couldn't go.

Life, coupled with human nature and its cruelty, can be so frustrating at times. It reminded me of the little girl in Nicaragua who cried because she had no school uniform and other children made fun of her. I told the mother that I would take the twins another time and it would be just the three of us.

* * * *

All the kids in the pueblo would soon know my favorite hang out which was the small hole in the wall fish fry. It was almost like a Coney Island stand where they would sell deep-fried fresh fish "catch of the day" together with French fries, and they were the best. I could have subsisted on this alone for my entire stay in Chile.

The kids all realized, very quickly, that if they could be there at the same time it was always my treat. The fish and fries were only a few pesos. I think I may have started the concept of a local hangout in the pueblo.

* * * *

Chile was entirely different from Nicaragua. It was excruciatingly beautiful in topography, scenic on the ocean, and rich in culture and diversity. The best part was the food.

Not only does Chile grow and export the most abundant of fruits and vegetables but also has an incredible selection of fresh fish. Because the coastline of Chile is in excess of 2000 miles, and the variety is vast, the Antarctic cold water keeps the fish the freshest.

However, one thing I could not get used to was the tongue of the sea urchins. They had the most sickening taste to me but every one there seemed to consider them a delicacy.

My favorite seafood was the mussels, which the fishermen would take out of the shells, place in an old tire intertube along with sawdust and then beat on the ground. This was done to tenderize the meat and was quite entertaining to watch.

In addition, Chile is one of the leaders in export of beef. The food was intoxicating and prepared in ways very European and different from the U.S. and, because it was so heavy into beef, goats and lambs you could also get the most wonderful cheeses.

Another thing I came to love is the bread. It is baked twice daily and bought daily in many varieties. Because the bread is always fresh, there is no need for the preservatives and additives used in most American bread products. When you first got the hot bread and put the fresh butter on it, it would melt in your mouth and you would think you had died and gone to heaven. However, by day two you could use the bread as lethal projectiles or build a brick house with them.

The market days, like Europe, was twice weekly on Wednesday and Saturday when you can buy fresh vegetables and other products. Almost everything in the country is fresh and then marketed on the main street so the need for preservatives or grocery stores like we know them are not needed and just an added cost.

You would often hear the milkman go by the house calling out; "leche de vaca" which means "fresh milk" and you could get milk from cows or goats. Chile is truly a health nuts' dream place to live and

because Chile is world famous for its wines, I guess it is
also a wino's dream come true.

Chapter 15

Casa De Menores

Anyone visiting the Casa de Menores was amazed by the size of the institution. It occupied about a city block with buildings in a very old architectural style with huge stone blocks of two-foot thickness, gray in color and rising two or three stories. The walls surrounding the complex were about twelve feet high. The place looked somewhat like a penitentiary yet governmental in nature.

The facility looked out over the ocean and you could smell the salty breezes. On the front end were the administrative offices and to the right was the older male section, which housed males from the ages of ten to eighteen.

Going through the center to the back section, was accessed by lock and key. This was the younger male section, which housed boys from the ages of six to nine. Each of the male sections had their own soccer field adjacent to the dormitory facilities.

The younger male section had roughly thirty five to forty five boys, most of whom had been abandoned. Because these boys were docile and non-threatening in behavior, they were cared for by two female counselors.

The older section had roughly ninety boys and was generally hardcore adolescents having been caught stealing, with drugs, and more serious behavioral problems. They were cared for by three or four male counselors.

To the left of the compound was the female section that housed infants and girls ages six to eighteen. The ratio of boys to girls was about two to one. The girls were allowed to help with the infant section that was a part of the female section.

The female section usually had four full time counselors on duty and cared for roughly sixty to eighty females. The infant section had two full time counselors to care for the roughly ten infants.

Both sections, male and female, were not allowed to mix, or dine in the eating hall at the same time. Each of the sections had a TV, some playing cards, a few very worn out books and two soccer balls. If one was not watching TV or playing soccer there was little else to do except wait for mealtime.

The soccer balls would not last very long with that much activity so many days the kids would substitute a rock for the ball, and continue playing. It really was quite amazing to see a rock about the size of a baseball being flipped around by there feet. A good day would be someone bringing a tin can in lieu of using a rock.

* * * *

After a couple of months of having the children brought to me for psychological testing, I decided that the center was not accomplishing its mission. This was to diagnose the children, recommend placement to a permanent center, and follow up after placement. I noticed that some of the children, particularly a number of the younger boys, had been at the institution more than three years.

The reasons given by the social staff was due to a lack of institutions, lack of adoptive parents, and no identifiable or reliable relatives, so the casa had no other choice but to maintain them.

This appeared to me to be a problem worth solving. The trick would be to stay within my guidelines, which were that it had to be accomplished with little or no money and by showing the nationals how to do it. Otherwise, I was not worth my weight in Peace Corps value.

I reviewed the files on all the boys in the young male section and decided to start there, as it seemed to need the greatest attention. I got a key and started to visit the section daily to observe the routine and talk to the children. I saw within days that the low IQ scores were more likely due to a problem of social deprivation than lack of intelligence.

I went about my investigation in what I thought was a non-intrusive way and not very obvious to the counselors or threatening to their purpose. I became friends with many of the children by learning their made-up and self taught games using rocks and sticks which were the only things in supply. I also told stories which the children and I both just loved.

The counselors enjoyed this because it added something more to their day than just supervising the children's getting up and getting dressed in the morning, through the meal routines, and back into bed at night.

After about a week of story telling I asked the children if any of them had a story they would like to share with everyone. No one volunteered so I took a bold step and asked the autistic child, who would win my heart and who had been at the center the longest. Some of the other children commented right away that Ernesto didn't know anything but rocking and spinning things.

Rocking back and forth for hours is a trait of autism in which the child escapes into his own world. Ernesto would also take any object placed in front of him and spin it like a top.

He was so adept at this that no matter what it was, it would soon be spinning. The two of us got into a competition. I would bring an object that I thought was nearly impossible to spin and he would invariably give it a whirl! For Ernesto it was exciting every time he saw me arrive because he knew I would have something for him.

I remember saying that I bet Ernesto had a special story that he shared only with himself and that it would be my honor and privilege to hear it. Ernesto got the biggest smile on his face as he stopped rocking and, to everyone's' amazement, cited the following:

> "Un bello globito de un color rojo
>   subiste subiste a ver el sol.
>   Yo no se que paso, el hilo se corto.
>   Un bello globito se desaparesio."

The English translation would read, "A beautiful red balloon flew up to see the sun. I don't know what happened, I guess the string broke. A beautiful balloon disappeared." That moment was a heart twister for me and once again that inner compelling need to help those children surfaced.

In two weeks, I determined that these children needed on site educational instruction given that they should be leaving after a year of evaluation. I had to figure out how to find the materials, write the training manuals and teach the counselors how to teach the children.

After discussions with the other psychologist, and briefing the staff, all agreed with me except for one minor problem, no money. The institution was operating based on the state budget for which no other funds aside from its primary mission were available. I would have to come up with my own solution but would have the volunteer services of one of the counselors on a full time basis.

Roxana, one of the female counselors was asked to assist me and given a chance to work with the gringo, while working on her university degree in childcare, seemed ideal to her.

I was as content as could be because I knew this would push my creativity to the level it needed to be pushed. I had a helper, and by God, I was going to do something to push the norm beyond what was normal around there.

16

Making Something Out Of Nothing

Roxana had no clue what I was about to put her through. In the beginning, she was highly embarrassed but I had already decided that if kids could invent games with sticks and stones, imagine what a child psychologist could come up with using trash.

I told Roxana that our first two weeks was going to be centered on just collecting trash, so if she could just accompany me, and help carry home the gold, which would be a great beginning.

Our first stop was a canvas canopy center, which fabricated the awnings used in front of stores and which were usually rolled down to block out the sun. We hit gold right out of the shoot! After explaining who we were, that it was not cash donations we wanted, but rather the trash, they were more than accommodating. What surprised them the most was that I didn't bother to embarrass anyone by only sorting out the best scraps but took it all! We had to make about three trips but got lots of heavy canvas material in the brightest, most colorful reds, greens, blues, yellows and oranges. Some of the scraps were as large as about eighteen inches square.

Our next stop, which Roxana absolutely detested, was the local hospital. I was sure they must have lots of goodies but all we walked away with was empty plastic kidney dialysis bottles, which I thought would be ideal for something.

From there we went to factory after factory. Even the local cookie company, after hearing our story and seeing our bags of loot, chipped in with several very large and full bags of broken cookie pieces. Just goes to show, most everyone has some throw-aways no matter what they make.

At this point, Roxana and I had to give the collection process a rest because we ran out of storage room at the center. All the counselors were starting to talk about the gringo and how he really needs some therapy himself. Management staff was starting to give me the impression that word was getting around town that the center was desperate and in need of, yes, even garbage.

I knew for this to be successful I needed to demonstrate, and fast, just what I was up to. I started first with the canvas. Roxana and I got scissors and started cutting one square, triangle, circle and rectangle out of each color of the canvas fabric. I explained to Roxana that, with these, we could teach basic colors and shapes. After sewing some of the shapes together and filling them with a variety of substances, we could also teach tactile development.

Roxana was finally sold on the idea. We then got busy searching through the garbage for things we could use to stuff the pouches. We had every thing from talc powder to toothpaste to marbles. Roxana and I would think up teaching games, notate them, and type them into a manual that could be used by the counselors. I even used the dialysis bottles! We filled them with different colored water, at different levels, and would then invent games, like trying to place the bottles in order of level and by color. The idea being, to do it in the least amount of time. This was great for hand-eye coordination.

By the end of the second month we had over 300 toys and games with multiple learning instructions for each. We assembled them all on tables in the cafeteria and invited the staff of the center to come and see the manuals and games. The staff could not believe their eyes. They seemed impressed that each piece was built to sustain many hands roughly handling them many times. They were really amazed at the fact that we had done all of this with only the cost of some glue and thread.

From that moment on, no one questioned our bringing home any more trash. Even the social workers started bringing in items they were given as a result of discussing this with other friends or other social workers.

One of the other Peace Corps volunteers heard of this via word of mouth and asked if we would put our display on loan with the local YWCA, which we agreed to do. I was then asked to come back and teach classes at the YWCA on infant development using these tools.

The next phase that Roxana and I put together was a battery of tests for the children which would be used to determine the effectiveness of the program. Very few of the children required testing because this was done as part of the on-going requirements of the center. It was mostly a matter of gathering the data and waiting to see what the post testing results would provide.

The director of the center allowed us to fix up and occupy space that was no longer being used in one of the buildings. This area was on the upper floor of the building that housed the younger boys. This was ideal, and we used several of the older boys to get the facility in shape.

We transferred the games we had up to the room and really decked out the place. It truly looked like the most bizarre toy store you could ever imagine. There was every thing from toy airplanes made out of film spools and Popsicle sticks which had numbers both written and in dots on each wing to teach math; colorful, shaped, pouches filled with things to stimulate the imagination, to weights made from sand in plastic bottles to improve manual dexterity.

When the first groups of children were brought up to the room to start the process, their eyes just sparkled. The counselors, whom we had trained, made sure order was maintained and chaos did not ensue. After six months on the program we tested the children again and saw a vast improvement in scores. It was not a scientifically controlled experiment, but logic dictated that to take children with nothing to do all day and introduce them to educational play material would have been the reason for increased scores and not osmosis from sitting on the dirt.

This program showed that the center was taking a proactive role in the development of the children. It made the days seem shorter for both the kids and the counselors and we did it all for the cost of glue and thread!

Here There And Everywhere

My bus ride from the house to the casa was taking me nearly an hour every morning because I Lived on the other side of Vina del Mar. I would have to bus to Vina, through it, to Valparaiso. On those bus rides I would witness some of the most humbling experiences.

I would often hear someone ask permission to sing. It may have been a mother or daughter, father or son, family or just an individual needing food money. In many instances, singing to those on a bus, or selling penny candies, for whatever money might be tossed their way, would be a family's only source of income. They realized that what they were doing was just a step away from begging but with pride barely intact, they had to do what they could to provide for their families.

To put it into perspective, imagine if tomorrow you had to sell pencils, or get up in front of a bunch of strangers on the metro or a street corner and sing songs without the benefit of an instrument and no singing skill. How humiliated would you feel? If your children's food depended on it I bet you could, I bet you would.

* * * *

I had promised myself to remain "apolitical" but within a few months I was even chanting under my breath "por una Chile liberada una guierra prolongada" which translated into "for a free Chile a prolonged war". I could not understand how a country of only twelve million people and an untold amount of natural resources could embody so much poverty. Chile was exporting one-third of the worlds copper and all sorts of additional metals and minerals. The country had cattle, fruits, vegetables, and the list just goes on and on. I would be floored to find that a few very fortunate individuals, who were enraged when Chile became the first country to elect a socialist government under Allende, hold the vast majority of all this wealth. Of course, these same individuals became instrumental in helping the Central Intelligence Agency and military overthrow the government. The problem now was that the corrupt dictatorship was worse than anything else.

The government had a program called "empleo minimo" which was, in my opinion, sanctioned slave labor. It would be looked at as a "social security" type of program whereby one was assured work, but at a wage that was only a few dollars a day, and for most families allowed them to purchase bread and tea. Most industries knew this and kept their wages low so that one would accept whatever they offered because the alternative was a full day of work for "pleo minimal".

The other thing that would outrage me was that every one in the country had to have an identification badge, even the Peace Corps volunteers. During my assignment President Pinoche decided to show the world that he did not have to give in to democracy and planned on staying in power until he died.

To show the world that the Chilean people were supportive of this, he decided to hold a "Plebiscite" where the people could go out and vote him a show of confidence. No other candidates were listed mind you, but each Chilean was requested to vote "yes" if they wanted him to continue or "no" if not.

To vote you had to show your identity card, which meant the record would show how you voted and who you were. The people were afraid to vote "no" because they knew they would be listed by the military and to not vote was a show of no confidence. Unless you were asking for trouble, you had to vote "yes". To make matters even more ridiculous, the ballot had a huge "yes" and a tiny "no" box and was designed to be intimidating by nature.

* * * *

I would not be able to stay with the current family for more than the first six months due to some delicate occurrences. The first was when the fifteen year old girl next door got drunk one night and Rene, the boy in our house, decided it would be a good idea to let her sleep it off in my bed.

I was in the small living room reading when I heard some one pounding on the front door with the force of nearly breaking it down. I jumped up and opened the door to see the next-door mother push me aside and charge into my bedroom.

No matter how much I tried to explain that I was not in there with her, the mother was so charged that I knew I was going to have to find Rene and get this settled. The last thing on my mind was to take on jailbait in a foreign country.

There were other incidences to follow that made living there impossible aside from the lengthy bus rides.

This would cascade me into a renting frenzy. The next week I secured a room close to the Casa de Menores but was not too pleased with it because it had no windows, had a funky, musty smell and was dark and drab.

I lasted only two months there because no matter how well I covered myself at night I was waking up and putting my hands on my back where my kidneys were and they would be ice cold.

It only took a few weeks for me to end up with continuing infections and weekly routines of antibiotics. I knew I had to get out of there before the nightmares started of waking up to find myself in a bathtub of ice, a bloody knife next to me and a sign hanging on my neck, "sorry took your kidneys you might want to get to a hospital". My next room was no better and while it had a window, I was renting from

Mrs. Bates, the mother, from the movie "Psycho". The first week there I found myself running into the hallway at about two in the morning in my underwear because there was screaming and hollering as if someone was being killed. There in the hallway was the old lady in her nightgown with a kitchen knife in her hand.

I ran up to her totally ready for anything but was amazed that she was asleep. I had never in my life heard of sleep walking of this caliber and screaming. She was confused when I woke her and then, of all things, she was mad at me. This would go on at least twice a week. It got to where I would put the chair against the door, to keep her from acting out her drama on me some night, and put the pillow over my head to drown her out.

Finally, half way through my assignment, I did find a room that had a balcony and was light and pleasant to be in, of course I paid through the nose but it was worth it.

18

A Friend For Life

I put the idea of any hopes of a social life out of my head because of the complications I thought it would cause dating someone at the center. Roxana however, was determined to be the matchmaker.

In February of 1979, I had taken notice of one of the female counselors, Gloria, who worked in the female section of the complex. She had a dark complexion, long black hair down to her knees and a face that could launch a thousand ships. So I made arrangements with Roxana to help me get invited over to the female section for whatever excuse we could come up with.

Like a trooper, Roxana was finding more reasons for us to go over there but it was hit and miss whether Gloria would be there. Sometimes Roxana would send a note over to the female section stating that the psychologist wanted to see one of the girls and if Gloria would escort her over.

For Roxana this was one gigantic game and had Gloria known what was going on, she would have died of embarrassment and probably would have had nothing more to do with me. Even the walls had ears at the center so the staff figured el gringo had zeroed in on one of their own, which was true, and they were ecstatic about it.

As luck would have it, and as natural as could be, Gloria and I ran into each other at one of the bookstores downtown. She invited me to "once" which is usually tea or coffee around the hour of three (a Chilean custom similar to English teatime) and we walked and talked until we got to her house.

Chile is quite like San Francisco in topography so most houses are built into the hills of the mountainside. It seemed like Gloria lived at the top of the mountain and walking up the winding sidewalks would wear out even the best marathon champion.

From that moment on we were close friends and she helped out with the sewing and gluing of the tactile stimulation games with Roxana and me.

We kind of fell into dating and I became a permanent fixture at her house. I still really didn't have any thoughts beyond dating but that would change dramatically in the course of my assignment. While our relationship moved from one of friendship to dating, we had discussed the fact that it shouldn't go any further.

The difficulties of two people from totally different countries being married seemed insurmountable. We were content with the way things were, and probably because of that, there was no pressure to progress to the next step.

Gloria and I were inseparable and her family became my adoptive home until December of 1979 when I took an R&R trip home to spend Christmas with my parents in Washington, D.C.   I did not want to spend another Christmas like the last two and because the R&R trip was a use or lose, I decided the best thing to do was go home.

Gloria saw me off at the airport and seemed cheerful enough but, just the same, it was a tearful good bye. As for me, I had the most lonely, empty feeling I could ever remember. It occurred to me that this was what I would feel like leaving her again in less than a year when my assignment would be over.

* * * *

Christmas at the Casa de Menores was depressing enough, and a sad time, so an opportunity came my way to at least make it a little more enjoyable for the little girls over in the female section. A friend of my sister Dawn, who lived in Minnesota, wanted to teach her young daughter the spirit of giving to those less fortunate.

My sister told her about me serving in the Peace Corps and working at the Casa de Menores. The mother took her daughter shopping and told her to pick out the one gift that she, herself, would like to receive for Christmas. The toy had several dolls, a little house and other accessories that would have lent its self

to being played with by more than one child at a time.
They wrapped it up and sent it to me to give to the
Casa de Menores. When it arrived, I was notified by
customs that I needed to come get it and that I had to
pay duty on it. I explained that I was a Peace Corps
volunteer and that it was for the little girls in the Casa
de Menores, but the customs agents remained
unimpressed.

After paying an outrageous amount of tax on
the shipment, I was devastated to find that probably
two thirds of the pieces to the toy had been stolen. Mail
tampering was not something I was used to!

* * * *

During those two weeks of R&R at Christmas, I
never once thought about getting married. What I did
do was go out and buy a three piece suit to take back
with me, which made absolutely no sense at all, given
that my jeans and boots were standard fare. Destiny
had to be taking my hand as I bought this suit with no
conscious thought as to what I would do with it, why I
was taking it with me, or why I expended the cost.

Upon arriving back in Chile, I immediately
went to Gloria's house, excited to be back and with
fresh enthusiasm for my work. While we were talking
about other things, I just proposed! I made a promise
that if she would marry me and come to the U.S., I
would fly her home once a year to spend time with her
family, a promise to this day I have been unable to
keep. However, we both seemed to know that this was
to be and she accepted.

I announced to Peace Corps what my intentions were and they approved. Something most people may not know is that when you are on a Peace Corps assignment, something out of the ordinary (like getting married) requires their consent. We had set a date for May 30, 1980. Peace Corps personnel assisted us with getting Gloria a green card via the embassy. Some volunteers do marry other volunteers but I was going outside the norm by marrying a foreign national.

Because Gloria was also working at the Casa de Menores, we looked for another place for her to work. She soon found a job at another center, the Centro Attencion Diurna (CAD), still working with children.

Our engagement really didn't impact our work at the casa much because I was in the young male section and she worked with the girls, it just seemed the right thing to do. In addition, I was spending more time working, at various centers in the area, in testing and placing the children.

I had agreed to go to a center in Vina del Mar. The name of the center was Hogar Teresa Cortes Brown. My job was to do free diagnostics at the center for run away and abandoned girls who were aged six to sixteen.

The center was having a specific problem with one fifteen year old that they were getting ready to return to the Casa de Menores because of inability to deal with her behavior. This young female had threatened some of the counselors physically, and according to the counselors, was demonstrating lesbian tendencies toward some of the other girls. While at this center, I was blown away by the conditions, and need for renovation and additional space. I left there with a lump in my throat knowing that something had to be done. I returned two days later and with the centers' permission took numerous photos and started writing up a proposal to try to get help.

I had been successful in Nicaragua so had the feeling that, given my analysis and photos, someone via the Peace Corps Partnership program would want to fund the project. My major worry, after getting my numbers together, was the excessive cost. I knew it was too high to be funded through the program so returned to the center to see if there was some other way we could get additional funding. The center found someone willing to match what I could come up with provided it did not exceed five thousand U.S. dollars.

The director of the center and I sat with a number of construction personnel, and with some pleading and persuasion, managed to find a company willing to do the construction at minimal labor cost, provided we supplied all the material. It turned out that the construction crew worked on their off hours and got paid next to nothing to help out.

This was ideal for them because we did not interfere with their wage earnings during the day and yet they earned a little more and felt good about what they were accomplishing in the evenings and weekends. The center would have to accommodate the workers with meals and put up with the construction efforts during odd hours but it seemed worth the effort.

I was right about someone seeing the situation as it was. The faces of the little girls in my photos got my funding quickly to renovate and add an additional

30-bed extension to the facility. We renovated the rooms that were there and added on the balance of space needed, which placed two girls per room and supplied an additional restroom.

I decided to be a little bolder and ask Peace Corps if they would consider supplying a volunteer to help the center. They did and a female volunteer named Ruth was assigned.

* * * *

Just after Gloria and I were married, we rented a room in the house adjacent to where her parents lived. The room was large, about 12x12, it had a small window to let the light in and most importantly it was close to home. The only problem was that it was the middle of winter in Chile and the room had no heat. Chile lies south of the equator so the seasons are opposite of ours in the U.S.

The temperature during the day doesn't get too bad, but at night it can dip down into the forties which can feel pretty chilly when you are use to a milder climate.

To make matters worse, the room had an old doorway on one side that was missing the door and boarded over but still had half-inch gaps to let in lots of cold air. I had bought an electric heater but it didn't do much good and kept blowing fuses in the rest of the house.

Gloria's father was able to get his hands on some thick, heavy cardboard and I plastered that over the opening.

I know this scenario may sound deplorable to some, but we were young and in love and things like that were more of a challenge than a nuisance.

* * * *

Both Gloria and I worked so we decided to use one of the local ladies in the area do our laundry and ironing. Her name was Maria and she appeared to be an elderly lady with a slow but genteel nature. We would always make sure she got something to eat if it was around mealtime or tea and bread if around "once". We took a real liking to her, as did Gloria's mom and dad so she became a regular around the house. You could tell she enjoyed being around us and I think she took her time to spend more time with us.

One day out of pure curiosity I went to see where Maria lived. It was one of the poorest houses that I would see in Chile. It was very dilapidated, very small, and without any amenities.

Maria lived with her mother and had no brothers or sisters. It was easy now for me to understand why her arms and legs were so badly scarred, why her clothes were so worn, old and few.

Because I am a curious person by nature this would spark a series of questions for which I was in total shock to hear the answers. The most shocking of those was to find out that what I thought was a poor, older woman, was really a young girl only the age of my wife, who at the time was only 22. It did not seem possible at first because of the stoop of her body, the white hair, the wrinkles and look of age in her face brought on by her hard life.   There are many people in this world today that like some of our ancestors, find themselves expended after a mere thirty to forty years of life.

I can't think of a sadder thing than the loneliness a young girl must feel knowing there will never be a prospect of marriage, the sounds of children and the fulfillment of keeping a home of her own.

I would later return to Chile with my wife and first born when he was about five years old and experience one of the greatest joys a father can have for his son.   Even though my son was born here in the States and grew up with all the comforts most kids do here, he looked beyond the physical appearance and poverty, and saw Maria as the kind, loving person she was and would always hug and play with her.   For Maria, playing with my son seemed almost like an escape back to her own childhood or maybe gave her a feeling of what it might have been like to have a child of her own.

* * * *

Shortly after Gloria and I were married, I decided my new family needed a pet! Or rather "pets" as it turned out. Earlier I had visited a llama farm with Roxana and fell in love with those animals. They were so gentle and adorable I just had to have something.

I don't always think in terms of practicality and rather than a common cat or dog I spied something at the market that I just had to have. Gloria's mom and dad are so easy going that they tended to let me do just about anything I wanted and I felt so comfortable in their home that I just did things with little or no discussion.

I convinced my new father-in-law this wasn't as bad as it seemed and he even helped out by bringing home some plastic liners so that I could create a makeshift wading pool for our "ducks"! I'm sure they thought I was whacky but those little things were so soft and cute I couldn't resist.

Now, I had never raised anything other than dogs and cats but I knew this would be fun. When the ducks were little fluffy, yellow chicks, they were quite a sight swimming across their little pond. When they got big and wanted to fly it was understood why some animals belong on a farm!

I was enjoying my wife, my family, and my job so much that I never wanted it to end. However, as the final days of my assignment approached the reality set in that I knew transition would now need to take place. I would need to leave all this and return with my new wife to the U.S.A.

Chapter

19

My Tuxedo Friend

In Valparaiso, I would walk the beach a lot because I loved the smell of the salty air, listening to the fog horns on a misty morning, seeing the ships disappear on the distant horizon and making the white lightening in the sand just after the water washes away.

I once tried swimming during the hottest part of summer but could not take the coldness of the water. The Antarctic waters flow along the Chilean coast so, no matter what time of year, the water is freezing.

The undertow was scary because the South American coast is what geologists call a sub-duction zone where one crustal plate dives down under the continent. Because of this, the relief of the underwater drops quickly and frighteningly down.

One day while walking on a secluded beach, I noticed what looked like someone or something farther down the beach.   I just casually walked on until I happened to notice that what was on the beach, was none other than a penguin.   He or she was short, dumpy and yes, the most adorable critter one could ever imagine. I got as close as I could, which was about six feet away, until it started to waddle off.

Figuring I was scaring it because of my size, I sat down in the sand. When I sat down it stopped and cocked its head at me and made the sound penguins do when they are communicating.

Wanting it to stay and not be afraid, I tried to mimic its sound, which seemed to work as it waddled over to me keeping its head constantly cocked to eye me. It was so well groomed and fluffy you just wanted to run over and hug it.

I did not leave until it decided I was not one of them, or had no food, whichever the case, and waddled out to the water and disappeared in the crest of the waves. I would ask around if that was common and found out that they nest just off the coast of Chile by migrating from Antarctica to the famous Robinson Crusoe Island, for which the classic book, "Robinson Crusoe" was written.

* * * *

Chile was truly an adventurer's paradise. I took the opportunity to go south to a very rustic Chilean port city on a Peace Corps retreat and experience the real native culture of Chile.

I would have the opportunity to see up close one of the world's largest structures, an oil drilling platform being towed to the seas of Norway. It was so large that it could not fit through the Panama Canal and would have to go all the way around the cape and back up the eastern coast of South America.   I could just imagine what a sight it would be in the rough waters around the tip of the continent because this was one of the most dangerous travels old time shipping could make.

I would witness a tropical storm so intense that it lifted a complete cargo ship and placed it on the beach. There is no sight more awesome than the seas of a huge storm and watching and listening to the waves batter the coastline.

I figure that the person who came up with the TV commercial "Join the Navy it's not just a career it's an adventure" must have spent time in Chile. This is a country that is truly blessed.

20

A Farewell Gift

As the time drew to a close with my assignment, the Hogar Teresa Cortes Brown project was complete. The psychosocial stimulation program was self-supportive and fully operational with the counselors. I had tooled back going to local schools to work with the children in Valparaiso and a strange finality to it all started to set in.

Roxana decided to leave and went to the campo to be with her future husband. The social workers stopped by to tell me how much they would miss me and that things would seem drab around there after I was gone. They got used to me singing Guantanamera and poking fun at my gringo accent.

When the final day came we had the normal farewell speeches, a cake and special meal was given for my send off. At the end, the director stood up and said, "Kirk, we have a special gift for you that while you can't take it with you, we feel you will enjoy it just the same". Besides, they said, I was taking the Glory out of Chile as it was. This was their humor about my taking Gloria back to the states.

To show you how well they came to know my personality, and me they came up with the greatest gift of all, and they knew it. They presented me with the notice that they had made arrangements to place Ernesto in a home. The tears flooded my eyes.

After Ernesto had waited more than three years, his ship had finally arrived. I asked if he had been told yet and they gave that honor to me. I could not and will not forget the smile on his face as I told him, and for the first time I could ever remember, he stopped rocking.

* * * *

I spent the final couple of weeks of my assignment processing out with the medical and dental exams and the final paper work. I felt my heart sink as I saw the new batch of trainees at the center all excited and filled with that determination to do something good and for which I was about to leave.

My assignment was at an end. It seemed I was taking home a bride from Chile, and Nicaragua not wanting to be left out, sent me home with its own remembrances.

The medical part of the processing out resulted in additional treatment for parasites, which I would need to continue with in the U.S.

Things had gone so well with my projects that my in-country support director asked me if I would consider extending my services for another year. I wanted to, and the Casa de Menores wanted me to, but I felt that I needed to now provide for a family and that I would be better able to do that in the United States.

I figured that I could earn more money and give my future children a better life. I had no concept of what it would put my new wife through to sacrifice her country, her family, her career, her language and her life.

My wife and I arrived in the United States in late October of 1980. Boarding that plane in Chile, with all of our relatives in tears, was one of the hardest things I ever remember doing. We were leaving the kindest, warmest, and most loving people I have ever known, to return to the dog-eat-dog world of Washington, D.C.

Almost immediately, I started substitute teaching at any elementary, junior or senior high school while looking for a permanent position with any one that would hire me.

Peace Corps kept aside, for volunteers, what they call a "readjustment allowance" which, at the time, was about $125 a month for every month served. So we had that little bit of money, which amounted to about four thousand dollars, and all our possessions, which we brought with us from Chile in four suitcases.

I applied for any and every kind of job but no one seemed to find value in someone coming from overseas. Regardless of all my Peace Corps accomplishments, I felt I was perceived by most potential employers as not being in touch with current events and with no relative experience for most U.S. jobs. Finally in January of 1981 two people, Tommy and Donna decided to take a chance on me. They hired me at the Washington Navy Yard to work in the Naval Weapons Engineering Support Activity in the Fighter Attack Division of the Navy as an Industrial Specialist.

Although I was hired at the lowest possible position and wage, many of the other workers were upset by the decision to hire me. They could not see where someone with my background could muster what it would take to do the job and that to go from the Peace Corps to the Department of Defense was, in their minds, a conflict of values.

I would go on to achieve Three Superior Performance awards in those first four years. I felt like I managed to prove myself to my co-workers but at great sacrifice because of the many extra hours spent trying to do what was, in its own way, no challenge compared to what I did in the Peace Corps.

I was 28 years old and did not make much money at first. We lived very poor as most couples do when first starting out. It was lonely compared to those Peace Corps years. We had given up our happy and content lives in Chile to live the "American dream" but found it fell way short of what we had left behind.

I cannot begin to tell you the number of times we longed to be back in Chile and how much I longed to be back in the Peace Corps. I would learn the tough lesson that money does not by happiness. I would also learn that having an executive job does not always mean job fulfillment. It was a hard transition to make. Looking back, it was one that need not ever have been made. I left the Peace Corps to pursue a new career, to make money, to provide a better education for my children. **I left the Peace Corps for all the wrong reasons.**

Chapter

21

A Life Complete

I have done many interesting things with my life since the Peace Corps. I have worked as an assistant production manager on the A-7 Corsair attack aircraft for the Department of the Navy. I actually saw them being machined out of a single block of metal at the Vought facilities in Dallas, Texas.

I have worked with the Navy's A-6 Intruder attack aircraft and gone with them down the assembly line with the F-14 Tomcats under fabrication by their sides. I have stood on the flight line and watched F-14 aircraft being hot refueled.

I saw the Space Shuttle Challenger wings being assembled and even the Grumman experimental forward swept wing prototype aircraft. I have worked with the Phoenix missile and the Light Airborne Multipurpose Helicopter and seen the first composite materials being made for aircraft wings and the use of night vision goggles. I have flown the F-18 Hornet Attack flight simulator, **but nothing I witnessed or did was as exciting as my Peace Corps years.**

* * * *

As the fall of the Soviet Union happened, I thought I could be of some benefit by working in the space program and went to work at the Kennedy Space Center. I worked with the launching of the Ulysses, which flew to the sun to study its poles; also with the Hubble space telescope, and had the chance to visit the clean room and see it up close.

I participated in the launches of Galileo to Jupiter, and Magellan to Venus. I helped with launch of COLBE, which gave us our first complete images of our own universe. I stood at the space center and saw the day and night launches of the Space Shuttle up close. I have gone to the top of the Vertical Assembly Building and seen the space shuttle moved to its pad.

I went on to help procure the world's largest robotic machines to fabricate a new space shuttle rocket engine **but none of this was as interesting to me as my Peace Corps years.**

* * * *

Finally, when it looked as if the numbers of those interested in space and saving the planet's environment was dwindling, I took up the cause by completing my bachelors and masters degrees in environmental science.   I have participated in the environmental cleanup of chemical, biological and nuclear wastes.

I have seen toxic sites and the new technologies being demonstrated to deal with containment and treatment of some of the most hazardous substances man could invent.   I have walked in fields of un-exploded ordnance and studied the design of chemical demilitarization equipment and facilities **but could not find the satisfaction I found while in the Peace Corps.**

* * * *

I have never worked as hard or for as many long hours as I did in the Peace Corps, and no one understands the Peace Corps phrase better than I that "It's the toughest job you'll ever love".

I have often thought that upon completion of the Peace Corps assignments, I could have died the next day as I felt I had completed a lifetime in just four years.

The End

ISBN 155369676-X